Just One Little Thing

Finding a Happy Life in an Imperfect World, One Moment at a Time

By Kelly S. Buckley

For the three men in my life.

For Brady, who supports and loves me without question or expectation, and makes all things seem within reach.

For Brendan, who teaches me every day and is the most resilient and compassionate person I know. I am blessed to be your mom.

And for Stephen, who continues to sit gently in my heart, and whose life on earth continues to ripple goodness every minute of every day.

You were a great gift, and every word I write is my thanks.

In the depth of winter, I finally learned that within me there lay an invincible summer.

~Albert Camus~

Introduction

Stars may be seen from the bottom of a deep well, when they cannot be discerned from the top of a mountain. So are many things learned in adversity which the prosperous man dreams not of.

~Charles Spurgeon~

Just One Little Thing started on the back of an envelope in the parking lot of a funeral home—truly, an unlikely start for a book about gratitude. It is an evolution of my first book, *Gratitude in Grief,* in which I wrote about finding daily thankfulness in the first two months following the death of my son Stephen on July 4, 2009.

My decision to revise some of the content of *Gratitude in Grief,* coupled with my unpublished writing, came after nearly a year of reflection on how I could continue to talk about having a thankful life in an imperfect world. Since the release of the book, I have received and responded to thousands of emails from people searching for a way through the most difficult of circumstances. I have been both touched and humbled by the amazing individuals who have contacted me, telling me that now they too are looking for their one little thing. It was through the letters from those readers that I realized *Just One Little Thing* needed to become a reality.

I've realized that a grateful, happy life does not arrive on your doorstep tied with a pretty bow. It's found in rediscovering the simple joys in the moments that can't be purchased. And most importantly, a life of gratitude can be found in less-than-perfect circumstances. In today's tumultuous world, this message could not be more important. We all have our struggles, and we all have a story to tell and could use a little help finding our one little thing to get us through. That is why I write.

This book captures my full journey, a snapshot of my first year without my son and how I forged a life of gratitude and purpose from one of the roughest of life's terrains. Joan Didion, in her book, *The Year of Magical Thinking*, wrote about the intense process of grief and loss as a period of wondrous thought. I wholeheartedly agree. I would add to that statement by saying that truly magical thinking comes from a connection that can only be found by surrendering to your circumstances, allowing yourself to feel the pain and letting the sadness wash over you like a heavy rain. I believe that surrender connected me to something much larger than my own mind, and during the year I write about within these pages, I was the most awake of my life.

I want to spark a conversation about the way we approach pain and loss. I believe we have convinced ourselves in this microwavable, instant message world of ours that recovery from difficulty should happen with the blink of an eye. Going further, perhaps we want to gloss over or medicate the difficulties in life altogether. We have this unspoken expectation that our lives should be perfect, and so it is no surprise that we are shocked when they are far from it. It is my hope that my approach to grief and loss may serve as a flicker of light for those who need it. I am asking that you consider the possibility that gratitude—even when it seems to be an unlikely companion during life's hard times—is, in fact, a healing elixir. What if I told you that the journey could be altered because of a decision to look for the goodness that still remains? What if there is a different way?

Finding a thankful life doesn't take away the pain. But it alleviates the suffering. And for me, that made all the difference.

Gratitude connected me to a Higher Source, something larger than myself, whispering in my ear, urging me to explore the possibility of hope. I am not afraid to admit that anymore. Throughout the book, you will see I use terms like God, Higher Source, even Big Guy (or Girl) in describing that Higher Power. I leave it open for you—the reader—to interpret that in a way that fits for you. I believe we all have different names for the divine, and that is okay.

As you read, you will notice that my reflections on life and gratitude evolve with the passing months. In the early days, my reality is raw; what I write about is equally as jagged. Each moment of gratitude I found could be viewed as a double-edged sword, as I moved in slow motion in a world I no longer recognized. With the passage of time, my reflections became more like storytelling. Rather than a chronological record of the good things I found in a day, I found gratitude in memories and contemplation. I began each day by finding a quote and have shared them in my account of this magical year. I've loved quotes for years, and each morning, the words of others served as a roadmap of sorts through my own difficulties.

My story is not unique or special. I now understand that the journey I write about is, in fact, universal. We all reach a point in our lives when we simply have no way out. And so, we must find the way through. I share my very personal and sometimes painful journey to let you know that you are not alone. And in the darkest of moments, there is always a measure of light. It is the balance of life.

My hope for you is this: As you read the final page, as you close this book and realize that no matter what your life situation, you can forge a happy life . . . one little thing at a time.

The Day Everything Changed

I look at life as a gift of God. Now that he wants it back, I have no right to complain.

~Joyce Cary~

"Hey, you," I said in a happy tone as I looked at the caller ID and answered my cell phone. It was the evening of July 4th, and the night sky was beginning to light up in Louisville, Kentucky, with people celebrating Independence Day.

The "you" I was referring to was my baby boy, my grown man, my pride and joy—Stephen. Having fun with his friends for the day, he'd decided to spend the 4th at Jordan Lake in North Carolina. Now he was 23, and I had watched him blossom over the past few years into an amazing man. A rising senior at North Carolina State University, Stephen was studying political science and looking forward to a bright future. My husband and I had discussed just the day before how happy and grateful we were, as he was having the time of his life. He had made some wonderful friends, and he was happy with the progress he had been making in his studies; he was just in a wonderful place.

But the caller on the other end was not my boy calling to wish us a Happy 4th. It was a Sergeant Barker, boating officer with the North Carolina Wildlife Resources Commission for Jordan Lake. I can remember knowing, as soon as I heard his voice on the other end, that my boy was gone. Although neither I nor he would say it, I knew it. As he spoke those unbelievable words, I thought back to my days as a nurse in Canada, working in the emergency department. I witnessed tremendous loss, seeing a physician break the news, the RCMP officers carrying the heaviness of death on their shoulders as they walked through the sliding doors of the ER. Or when I worked in the oncology clinic, talking to family, attempting to provide some measure of comfort when the gravity of their prognosis had been shared and all hope had slipped away. I had a membership to that club, the group that, because of their chosen profession, carries the burden of bearing witness to the fragility of life—the full spectrum of life, with all of its joy and the equal measures of pain. I, like many in the profession, would be there in the moment of tragedy, and then would have to look away and choose to move on from it quickly. To carry all of that pain with you for too long was simply too much of a burden to carry, too grim a reality to contemplate. That is why, when you watch reality shows about trauma units, you find that each employee has that edge, that dark sense of humor. It is a survival tactic to get you through what you see and experience within the confines of a 12-hour shift.

And here I was, on the other end of that message. The conversation was a blur of high-level information, directions to the lake, with Sgt. Barker planting the seeds of reality for this child's mother. As he spoke, I wondered if he had ever had to make this type of call before or if this was his first. I wondered if he practiced in his mind how he would say it. Once directions had been given and he had stated the facts, he paused and then quietly said, "And, just to let you know, we have been searching for Stephen for 30 minutes now." Ka-Boom! My life as I knew it simply imploded, blown to bits by this painful truth.

"30 minutes now."

That was all we needed to know, wasn't it? He was so respectful in the manner he presented that grave information, and because I had been in his position before, I knew that he had finished the call with me with a heavy heart. That phone call was the hardest part of his job, without a doubt. I wondered if he had a family, if he had gone home that night and kissed his children. Maybe he held them a little longer, a little closer, as I often did with Stephen after a particularly painful shift. I thought about his story and how, in his career, this would become part of it, a notation in the chapter about his professional life. I had memorable patients whom I will carry with me for a lifetime. The man getting ready to be discharged after months in the hospital recuperating from an accident, only to throw a clot as he put on his shoes. He died, right there in front of me, with one shoe on and one shoe off. He had worked so hard to recover, and in an instant, it was over. Another patient, he was a gorgeous teenage boy, one moment full of life and in the next gone after a freak accident that left him with a broken neck and his friend without a scratch. I can still remember every detail about him—the smell of his hair gel, what his parents had been wearing, the scent of his father's cologne, and the heaviness in the air as his family realized it was true: he was not coming back. I wondered if we would be a memory like that in the mind of Sgt. Barker or if our story would fade away with time.

It was almost comical how fast my husband and I readied ourselves to get on the road. Having just arrived home from a leisurely July 4th celebration, we were winding down for the day, stomachs full and hearts happy. Once the call came in, we sprang into action. Clothes were thrown into the suitcases, things were gathered quickly and pitched into the car, the dog was readied for the trip. Have you ever willed a dog to pee? It is no small task. With Brady's parents standing in their garage, looking at us with shock and concern, we left to drive 9 hours through the night to the lake.

They urged us to stay, not to drive off into the darkness in this emotional state. Thinking back, it was probably not the most sensible thing to do. But it was what we had to do. We needed to get to Stephen. The thought of sitting there, trying to find a flight as they searched for him, was simply too much to bear. I needed to be in action, taking some steps, however foolish, to bring me closer to my son.

As we drove through the night, passing one community after another, the fireworks filled the night sky on both sides of the interstate. Beautiful colors burst through the darkness and cascaded down until they disappeared into the earth—much like Stephen's life, a burst of beauty gone too soon. Perhaps the fireworks were not for independence this year but rather to welcome my special child into heaven. I had the thought and then banished it, not wanting it to be true. Stephen's welcome into heaven . . . I could not verbalize this analogy to my husband for fear I might will it into existence. The fireworks were coupled with rain, as if the heavens, celebrating his arrival, realized how many people would suffer once they heard the news and cried tears along with me for our agony. But as the minutes turned to hours, I realized that no news was, in fact, the worst news I could ever imagine. They had not found him on some shoreline, dazed and confused and injured. They had not found him at all.

At around 12:45 AM, we received a call from Sgt. Barker, explaining that for workforce and visibility reasons, they were calling off the search. They would resume in the morning. And, although I knew the reality of the situation, neither Sgt. Barker nor I could bring ourselves to say the obvious after hours of searching. The most he could utter to me was,

"You need to prepare yourself."

I was thankful for that, grateful that he had not announced that his search had shifted from rescue to recovery. I had often watched televised reports at crash scenes and wondered how families felt when that announcement was made on the evening news as they were sitting on their couch at home, glued to the television, waiting to hear some news about a life-altering tragedy. I wondered how it felt when someone with perfect articulation, coiffed hair, and whitened teeth takes all your hope away.

"You need to prepare yourself."

Tell me, Sgt. Barker. How does one do that? How does a mother prepare to be told her baby is gone? How do I prepare myself for what I will see when I arrive at Jordan Lake? How does a mother get ready to hear those words spoken, the words and thoughts every mother turns away from as they raise their children, too painful to even consider? Prepare yourself, he had said. So, we did. We called family in Canada with more calm than I would have thought possible, explained the situation, and told them to prepare themselves. Driving through the night, Brady and I expressed every emotion possible. We were silent and sad, chatty and anxious, crying and desperate, sentimental, and so damn logical it was sickening. We planned the funeral, the memorial, to the finest details, knowing in our hearts how we wanted to celebrate his life, or rather, how he would want his life to be celebrated. We really did know what needed to be done. We just knew, without a doubt or a second guess.

The road was dark and wet. I turned on the stereo to pass the time as we drove, to distract me from the painful reality that was my life. And as if Stephen had cued it up to be ready for us, a CD of his favorite tunes began to play. As the words of each song reverberated through the car, it was almost as if he was speaking to us, as if he was sitting there with us. I believe. I believe he was sitting there with us for each long hour through the night as we traveled the loneliest road, where the destination was heartache and loss.

I felt him. The rain poured from the night sky for almost the entire trip, letting up only when we were on the final road leading us to the lake. But I knew we would be okay. I knew that he was with us. For those who have not experienced a loss of someone you loved deeply, I know this may sound like the ranting of someone in grief, and I suppose to a point, it is. But he was with us, hand on my shoulder, there with us to help us through. And although I had never felt more distant from HIM, I knew God was with us too.

It was hard to know if the decreased visibility was due to the heavy rainfall outside or the tears streaming down my face. I continued to listen to his deep yet quirky music. I laughed, I cried. Haunting melodies ran through each song, the words speaking of young love lost, of going away, and of loving in spite of distance and time. Each song spoke of promise, told a story of who he was and what he envisioned for the next chapter of his life. And all I could think was, *God, it's me, Kelly. Take me. Please hear me, just take me. Leave him and take me.*

I negotiated throughout the night, silently.

While still in Kentucky, we passed a car and looked at the license plate on the rear of the vehicle. It read **One Lifetime**. Tears streamed down my face like a rainstorm on a window. *One Lifetime*—the words on the tattoo he had on his left flank. He'd decided to get the tattoo just three weeks after leaving for college, a rite of passage as he embarked into adulthood, he and his girlfriend. She had announced it to me when I went to visit. I remember the look on his face as she told me, as she was quite proud of it and had no reason to think I would be upset. Stephen, however, was desperately looking for an opening in the floor.

I have one eyebrow that rises when I am perplexed with a situation. That eyebrow has kept me honest through the years and has let people know exactly what my position has been on any matter. It did not fail me when she announced this tattoo. After the shock, I did not say much about it. He was, after all, a grown man capable of making decisions about his own life. *One Lifetime*—how absolutely poignant at this moment. *Are you speaking to me, Stephen?* How very appropriate that this should be inked on his skin. It was exactly how he lived. He knew he had only one lifetime, and he was the kind of person who made sure he fit as much in as he could on any given day. Was it a simple license plate or a message from him? I will never know, but that car followed us through three states as we drove in the dead of night, leaving us only when we took the exit for Jordan Lake.

As the minutes ran into hours, I had some deep conversations—not only with my husband but silently, with God and with Stephen. I reviewed every minute of my time with him. From the pregnancy, to growing up right along with him, I played out every celebration, every hardship, every heartache. And no matter what the stumble or new beginning, the depth of our love had been unchanging. I had only had one true argument with him—ever. Sure, there was always some eye rolling and some huffs, puffs, and sighs as a teenager, frustration at times with choices, or discipline. But we had only truly argued once in his entire life. It had been on New Year's Day two years prior, and it had taken me about 6 months to recover. He would smile when I brought it up and say, "It's okay, Mom. It is over. It was just an off day. We both love each other, right?"

Imagine that: only one argument. He had experienced a tough semester and was struggling to find his way, and we had both lost sight of the fact that we wanted the same thing: his happiness.

I questioned why I would have to experience the death of my own child, again, out of the natural order of things. I questioned why God would give me two children in one womb only to take them both away. As the night turned to morning, we drove the last stretch of road to the lake. I think driving would be a little inaccurate, as I remember us kind of flying over the pavement. As we moved past the shoreline, I realized just how big it was—a massive lake and beautiful in every way; I surmised that thousands must have enjoyed this place every summer. The water was blue and glistening, with wonderful, lush trees all along the edge. It looked to have a number of sandy coves around the perimeter. It was perfect.

We arrived at the spot at about 6:30 in the morning, and we were alone, as the search had not yet resumed for the day. There we were, my husband and I with our big, brown dog, Rudy. Walking ahead of Brady down the trail, I began to cry uncontrollably, sobbing and making this guttural sound as I walked along the water's edge. The last time I had made that noise was on the night of Stephen's birth. The setting now was serene and absolutely magnificent; it just didn't seem like a possible location for the end of someone's life, especially not Stephen's. He was an athlete. He ran for miles, climbed trees, pushed himself physically in ways I could only dream about. How could this picture-perfect setting be the place to take him? It simply did not make sense to me. After everything, being born 8 weeks too soon and all of the other struggles we had been through together, and he had been taken away because he had gone for a swim?

I was inconsolable, crying from the depths of my soul in the same way I did for his twin brother on the night of his delivery. It was dreamlike. I could hear the sounds coming out of my mouth, but they did not sound human. Wandering around with Rudy, I prayed we would find him ourselves before any search party or stranger. The water was like glass, and the trees still, not a breath of air. It was as if God had asked everyone to be quiet out of respect. And then, I saw it. One spot in the water, and for some reason, I could not take my eyes away from it. There was nothing to see, just still water and some gentle ripples from the fish moving below the surface. But I knew. I sat on a bump of sand in front of that spot, with Rudy by my side. As Rudy whined, he looked at the same spot as I did and scratched at the water's edge. Were we right? I will never know why, but I knew that was where they would discover him. And on their very first dive, that is exactly where they found my boy.

Sitting there, I repeatedly said the same words in my conversation with God. *Take me, please, God, just take me. Please, please God, just take me.* Over and over, I begged God to be merciful and to take me and leave Stephen on the shore to be found, alive, to continue with the promise of his life. The world could continue to turn without me in it, and Stephen had so much left to do. I thought about my other son and how I loved him but would be willing to sacrifice my own life if it meant I could bring back his brother. Oh, the ache. The physical and emotional ache that rocked me—I have never known anything like it before or since. Because the more I said those seven words, the more I realized that we were beyond choices, and there would be no negotiation.

I contemplated letting Rudy go in, but a sheriff was circling in her boat, looking at me with concern. She maneuvered closer to the shoreline and explained the plan for the search. She seemed young, so very young, and I could not figure out if she had children of her own. I did not think so. If she did, her breath would have caught in her throat when she tried to speak to me. That was, at least, how I had reacted in similar situations. She gently spoke to us about not being there when the divers arrived to begin the recovery operation. As she explained, it was not something a mother should have to see. As she moved the boat away from me, I could hear her talking to her colleagues on the radio and saying, "You guys, I understand, but this is his mother, and she wants to be over here."

They needed me to leave for fear of what I might see when they pulled him out of the water. It was surreal listening to that conversation. I wondered if any parents had heard me have a dialogue like that in the ER. To be discussed in the third person, your wellbeing and emotional state the topic, with everyone feeling they understood what was best, without you saying a word. The one piece of the puzzle they did not see or understand is what I'd had with him. They were being kind. I knew that, but did they really think anything I might see would make this situation any worse? Did they think anything I could possibly see could be any worse than what I had pictured in my mind for every hour of that drive? Did they think that anything that I could possibly witness could be more painful than the realization that my child was dead?

In any case, I surrendered to it. I am not a woman for dramatics, and so I agreed to relocate to where they were forming the search.

Arriving at the dock where the Search and Rescue group had set up their headquarters, I noticed that the police had closed the site to the media. We drove by the barricades, saying, "We are Stephen's parents." Dreamlike. Can't be. Pulling into the parking area, I lifted my head, and there they were. His friends, a group of lost souls standing there at the water's edge, as the rain fell gently on each of them. As we pulled up, the tears flowed freely, both from our eyes and theirs. Just weeks before, they had spent the weekend with us, lying on our couch, laughing, playing Frisbee golf, drinking our beer and eating our food, and we had loved every minute of it. Now, the looks on their sweet faces spoke of so much hurt and sadness. They looked older. Oh, how wrong, to have the joys and innocence of your youth taken away so quickly, and in this manner! I remembered that I had been a little younger than them when my parents had died, and it had forever changed me. I could see that same change in their eyes that morning.

They stayed with us at the shoreline. Their parents stood with us, strangers showing up at a lake on a cloudy Sunday morning for no other purpose than to offer comfort. They brought food, water, chairs, umbrellas, and love. Lots and lots of love. They stood right next to us during the most challenging time of our lives. And they did not look away.

The warm summer rain hit softly off the top of my head. It was the only thing that made me feel remotely alive. I watched the boats head off to the cove and out of my field of vision. And we waited.

And then they found him. The paramedic came to explain to me that they would be bringing him back shortly. She was an interesting sort. She had probably worked at her job for a few years and had more seniority than the obvious green and inexperienced colleagues who stood over next to the ambulance shuffling their feet and having nervous conversation. When I looked over, they looked away. She, however, did not. She came and introduced herself and explained what would happen. She was professional and very kind, but somehow, I felt she was patronizing. I think it was the smile. She was smiling as she explained things to me. I know that the smile was meant to show kindness and compassion, but it simply did not fit with the circumstances. She instructed me that they would need a moment to prepare Stephen before we could see him. I explained I would give her 7 minutes, and then I would come and help her. I told her I was a nurse, and I just wanted to see my boy. That tone, the tone of her voice and that damn inappropriate grin—I will never forget it.

The boat arrived, and they raised a sheet to cover the removal of his body. *This simply cannot be real.*

Finally, they allowed us to see him. We stepped into the back of the ambulance, and there he was. Sleeping perhaps, I thought. Maybe it was just a cruel joke; I could take the punch line if he sat up now and said he was sorry for deceiving me. But alas, it was not a gag. It was all too real. His essence, his spark was no longer with us. The connection I felt with my flesh and blood, my baby was not there in the same way it had been since the first time I had held him 23 years earlier. His spirit was gone . . . or was it? Or was it all around me, surrounding me like a warm sweater on a frigid winter night, hugging into my chest, giving me comfort and hope? Brady and I held our breath for a moment. Just inhaled and stopped. Time stood still. The world stopped its rotation for an instant. And then, it was a real. It is hard to describe that moment in simple words, so I will not try. I will not share every detail, as I don't need to. But it was the moment that I changed, Brady changed, our lives transformed, and our view of the world and life was forever altered. We took some time to say goodbye to his physical body, his sweet and handsome face, his perfect athletic physique. Farewell to the dreams of his future, of love and marriage and grandchildren and watching him continue to blossom into the amazing human being that he had become.

And so, the journey began.

How Do You Describe a Life?

Making the decision to have a child – it is momentous. It is to decide forever to have your heart go walking around outside your body.

~Elizabeth Stone~

1986. Things were happening way too fast. It was just weeks before I would finally tell my family about my pregnancy. Two weeks later, an ultrasound revealed I was carrying not one but two babies. And on May 21, 1986, I was staring with shock into the eyes of the OB/GYN resident standing at the foot of my bed.

She had bright red hair, cut very short, close to her head. I remember thinking that the haircut was not a matter of fashion for her but rather because she thought she was much too busy and important to manage any other style. She wore hospital greens and a lab coat, and with her stethoscope strategically placed around her neck, she marched around the unit like she was the smartest person on earth. She immediately rubbed me the wrong way, perhaps from my own fear of the unknown but more likely because of intimidation. She was a woman who wanted you to know she was the smartest in the room and seemed way too strong in the face of the weakest moment of my life.

I was lying in the same bed I had stayed in for the past 36 hours, in a darkened room, with little or no stimuli and hooked up to not one but two fetal monitors. Preeclampsia was the reason they gave to me for this solitary confinement. I would not understand just how serious that could be until years later, but I did know I did not feel right at all. I was alone when she arrived, and I wished that someone had been with me to somehow protect me from the abrasive tone in her voice, perhaps soften the impact of her personality on my fragile soul.

"I need to examine you," she said in a statement rather than posing it as a polite request. I was young but smart enough to know what she thought of me, a young girl in a hospital bed, pregnant but still in high school. I could feel her impatience with me when I asked why the examination was required; her body language spoke loudly to me of her frustration. She did not have time for me. She did not see beyond my bulging belly. Because of her impatience, she did not see that I was an honor roll student or that I could sing in a few different languages or that I had big plans that now sat on the unknown list. She chose to see none of it; I was simply a task in her day, not worthy of the respect she would later show the married, professional woman in the adjacent bed.

Finally, when I realized I would not get a response to my inquiry for the rationale of this examination, I simply complied. To this day, I think of that moment as a violation, not an examination. She took something from me in that moment: my dignity. I now realize her treatment of me affected the way I treated people in my own nursing career and in every aspect of the rest of my life. I would remember her disdain for me every time I pulled the curtain closed prior to examining a homeless man who was ravaged by the effects of alcohol and drugs in the emergency room, needing someone to help, even if only to get well enough to go out and do the same thing to his body all over again. I would remember her when I was tempted to judge someone on the basis of a first impression as something less than myself. It is said that the people who hurt and test you in your own life are actually your greatest teachers. And although it is still difficult for me to give this person any credit, I have to agree with that statement. She gave me a lesson I will carry with me forever.

Following her cold and indifferent examination, she announced to me, "You are in labor. Two centimeters dilated."

"No. I can't be," I said in disbelief. Still alone in the room with her, she rolled her eyes at me, bored with my ignorance.

"Well, you are. I will tell your doctor." And with that, she walked out.

I sat up and let my feet dangle off the edge of the bed, looking down and wondering where my ankles were vacationing, as I had not seen them in some weeks. My head was light and woozy, my blood pressure high. The shock of her words instantly upset my stomach. I was not ready for this. But I knew that she was right.

Even in my youth and inexperience, I knew that my body was telling me that it was time for these babies to come out, regardless of the fact that it was 8 weeks too soon. Some days earlier, I'd had such a foreboding feeling, yet I was unable to articulate exactly what was wrong. Standing in my parents' bedroom, tears streaming down my face, I could only say, "There is something wrong with one of the babies."

It was an unusual feeling, both a physical sensation of being unwell and a larger emotional sense of dread, an unexplainable knowledge of something I did not want to know. I prayed to St. Gerard, the Saint of Mothers. I prayed for a sick and dying child over and over again. I just knew.

Following the resident's unfeeling declaration of my fate, I stood staring into the bathroom mirror and looking at my very young reflection, knowing that birth was imminent. The girl in the glass did not look like a mother. She looked young and inexperienced. She looked very afraid.

And despite the fact that the fetal monitors recorded and printed a steady heart rate for both babies hour after hour, I had a strange feeling that this would not end well. But I didn't say anything. I kept silent, thinking maybe that this feeling of dread was related to my overall uneasiness about impending motherhood. I feared if I verbalized this dread, it would appear I was not being motherly or imply that I did not want the little ones inside of me.

This was my first experience with the maternal connection between mother and child. And although I did not realize that nor understand what it was to be motherly, my instincts were laser focused, and I knew there was something terribly wrong with one of my children.

Labor progressed as labor does. Some of the memories of that time are clear, and some are quite clouded, blocked out for my own comfort, recollections judged to be irrelevant in the telling of this story.

As I entered the next stage of active labor, so much was happening around me. There were muffled and hushed voices outside the room; I could hear their quiet conversations in the hallway, making preparations for the approaching birth. My family physician entered the room, and I exhaled; he was a familiar face and someone who had been respectful and had shown me human kindness regardless of my circumstances. I trusted him.

And in between the cleansing breaths, I said,

"That resident, the one that told me I was in labor, she's not allowed in the delivery room. I don't want her in my room ever again."

You see, as young as I was, I was still smart, and I was still powerful, although I had no idea what my personal power was, and that discovery would span my lifetime. I understood that this was probably an exciting event for her in her residency and would be something she could check off her list of experiences in her training. She had not taken this into consideration when she had marched into my room earlier that day. She needed someone like me.

So, as immature and naïve I was, I still listened to the quiet voice within me, the one pushing to ensure she was not one of the first human beings to look into the eyes of my children. *No, I thought, you will have to sit outside, you will have to go and sit in the cafeteria, maybe eat some pudding from a vending machine as I was delivering twins. And I hope you understand that your lack of empathy and basic human kindness is why you were shut out of my experience.*

Before I knew it, I was being wheeled into the delivery room. Lying flat, prepped for delivery, I was overwhelmed by the lights, the people, everyone waiting for the arrival.

Matthew, born first, arrived to a deafening silence. Looking around into the eyes of the masked faces, I searched for some recognition, some hint of information. But, as I looked to each of them, they averted their eyes, quickly looking away. The room was full, this twin pregnancy with someone as young as I was a rare event, I supposed. But as inquisitive as they all were, no one had the courage to make eye contact with me or answer my questions. The only eyes that met mine were those of my doctor's and my sister's. My sister's were tear filled, her voice was shaky, and all she could manage to say was that it was time to deliver the second baby. My doctor's eyes, although competent and supportive, showed a sadness that could not be hidden. No words were necessary. And even they could only look for a moment and then had to look away.

Knowing in my heart what that silence translated into for my life, I simply stopped; I simply could not do it. I could not bear the thought of delivering my remaining child only to have him snatched away as well. I hesitated, although now, thinking back, I don't know if it was simply a feeling of reluctance in my mind, as birth is an event much like death. You are not in control; it is a higher power that calls the shots on scheduling.

So, life continued to move on, despite my silent protest and request for it to stop. And a few short minutes later, Stephen Patrick Russell was born at 02:51 AM on May 22, 1986. And there he was.

Stephen came into life giving me comfort, filling my heart with joy from the beginning with his tiny little cry. Through the oppressive silence in the room, Stephen was able to do the one thing that no one else in the world could do: give me a joy for life and some comfort in death all in one cry, in confirmation of his presence. *I am here! I am here with you, and you are not alone,* Stephen announced to the world with a frail bellow. And my world would never be the same after.

I was a young girl, a child in so many ways, when he was born. I was not ready for the challenges of parenting. I had no clue what was to come. But there we were, together. As a pregnant teen, I had entered that hospital lost, at a fork in the road, unsure of which way to turn in my life. And as if God had answered my prayers, my roadmap for the rest of my existence had arrived.

Stephen spent a few weeks in the special care nursery prior to coming home. It was very overwhelming to go there for the feedings. Some of the nurses were adamant that a successful feeding was what I needed to bond with my child. I don't think they understood that I had bonded with him from that first cry, and his existence was connected to me much like an emotional umbilical cord.

He looked very breakable. He appeared extremely complicated. Between the life and death experience at his birth, a premature infant to care for, and my youth and immaturity, I had no idea how I was going to pull this off. I was tremendously lucky to have the family I did, to guide me and teach me how to care for him.

To call him an easy baby would be an understatement. He was just agreeable. Nothing fazed him. He understood when things did not go according to plan, and he rolled with the punches. Even as a toddler, if you told him not to do something, he simply didn't do it. I write that, knowing I sound like a completely biased mother, but it is true. I could not take any credit for such successes—no credit at all. I had no idea why he was that way, as I was, on the other hand, emotional and temperamental and learning this parenting thing as I went along. He had this way of comforting, of seeing the good in any situation, of finding peace in any circumstance, of knowing what people needed and giving it to them freely and without expectation of something in return.

He was a quiet but confident child. Many who met him thought he was painfully shy, but that was not the case. He was simply observing and did not feel the need to be at the center of the conversation. In some ways, I think he was watching to see who needed him, knowing that you sometimes can understand more about a situation by standing at the periphery instead of right in the middle. He, even in youth, was rare to make rash judgments of people. He loved family. He was, even up to the moment of his death, both street smart and painfully naïve at the same time. I so admired that, as it seemed like he had made a choice to be naïve about situations, a deliberate decision to simply see life with fresh eyes.

He was handsome, so very handsome, and athletic. But he did not know it. His athleticism came naturally and was accentuated by his willingness to try anything without the fear of stumbling as he learned and mastered new challenges. He was fiercely competitive, but the challenge was always within Stephen, not with others. In hockey, he excelled farther than he should have for only starting the sport at the age of 12. And I loved to watch him run; it was like watching the wind blow across a field of wheat. It was rhythmic and fast and beautiful. In everything that he did sports related, it was not that he was the best. It was simply that he decided not to give up.

He loved food, and he had an ability to put away more sustenance than seemed possible for his physical size. His grandfather joked that he had a hollow leg. It was a deep and long-lasting love affair with food, and it was truly something to watch when he sat to enjoy one of his favorite meals. He did not eat fast but painfully slow, and he ate things in order. So, he would eat the green beans first, then the potatoes, then the steak, and on and on. Never all together, but neat, tidy, orderly, and in massive amounts.

He did his own laundry from an early age. I never really understood it. He just did it. I oftentimes thought about being able to replicate that trait in other men in the world. If I could have figured that out, I could retire early. He also loved to clean. I would come home from work and the house would be spotless.

Children gravitated to him, and he would play with them as if he was seven all over again. He never had that ego, that feeling he needed to "act his age." On the previous July 4th, I had watched him play in the sand with a four-year-old for an entire afternoon.

He loved the Power Rangers and Mortal Kombat. But he also read Walt Whitman and wrote poetry. He loved music, all music, and had an eclectic taste and listened to everything from classical to hard rock.

He had a temperament that I could not take credit for; he always had a smile, was never quick to anger, and had vision that always saw the good in people and situations. Truly, he was a gentle and old soul.

He was a gifted artist, although no one knew it. He sketched and created in private, leaving a treasure of beauty behind that spoke of his deep thoughts on life and love.

These are all random thoughts, I know, but how else does one describe their child and all the delicious and unique traits of a person that gave them so much joy?

Our life was not without struggles, but for the most part, we had decided to be happy. We had both, without much conversation, decided to choose happiness. Looking back on it now, I never saw the true power of our own resilience. I never saw that his unconventional beginning was the very reason our relationship was so very exceptional.

All of it, the good and the bad, brought him to a sunny July 4th.

He was not perfect—no one is. But he was close. And to see him—my resilient, beautiful Stephen—it simply took my breath away. To see him be happy in the last few years of his life was the greatest gift a mother could ever receive. It is a gift I hold close to my heart.

Twenty-three years ago, a child gave birth to a tiny, beautiful miracle. I thought life was over, that I had no future or possibility. And years later, I would look back on that time and say it was the best thing that ever happened to me. I always called him my fork in the road, and he was.

Because of what he and God had taught me at his arrival, I know that something good always comes from the moments in life where you are brought to your knees with pain. I believe; I have to trust that just as with his birth, his death will lead me to a greater purpose, wiser and stronger.

Finding "Just One Little Thing"

She was no longer wrestling with the grief but could sit down with it as a lasting companion and make it a sharer in her thoughts.

~George Eliot~

One of the questions that I am most often asked is why I decided to grieve with gratitude as my companion. And although I would love to be able to respond with some thought-provoking, evidence-based answer on my rationale, I don't have one. To be completely honest, I'm just not sure why I decided or if calling it a decision would even be accurate.

I suppose I could say it had something to do with the lessons I had learned previously through heartache and loss. Stephen's very birth taught me about the balance that exists between life and death. I felt both tremendous sadness for the loss of one child and happiness and excitement over the birth of another all at the same time. The balance of happy and sad coexisted for every diaper change and every birthday.

My parents lived lives of gratitude—through their actions and service to others, their selfless parenting. Perhaps that example played a huge part in my decision to give thanks in the worst of circumstances. They were my first teachers, explaining that if you receive a gift, you should respond with thanks. So, I suppose I came into this life-changing event with a positive perspective. But to grieve with a focus on what was good?

I do feel one of the biggest reasons I began was the gentle whisper in my ear on the morning of July 5th. Sitting on the sand at the water's edge, waiting for the divers to find my boy, I just suddenly knew this would be what I needed to do. It was almost as if God or Stephen had made the recommendation to me, and I listened. I write this tentatively, knowing that in my earlier description of this time, I hesitated to elaborate too much on how connected I felt on that morning. But on that day and in the months after, because I said "yes" to the suggestion that came from a universe much larger than myself, I was linked to a wisdom and a certainty about life that I will never be able to explain adequately in the written word. I just feel so blessed that I decided to start writing.

I see every word I wrote during that year as a personal and healing conversation with my Higher Power.

I could see things clearly, and I had a sense of clarity about what mattered, what is not visible until life stomps you into the floor and then crushes you with its heel a little further just to make sure you can never be put back together in exactly the same way again.

Forever changed, I began to see things much differently. Things that once had tremendous importance fell away from my life. Things that should be truly valued were now illuminated. I still marvel at the fact that I could find some gratitude amid the worst event of my life. Something bigger than me pushed me to document this, and I believe I listened at that time because my heart was finally still, unmovable because it was simply shattered. It was as still as the water in that cove on that cloudy Sunday morning. And with that calm came clarity, an unexplainable knowing. I knew that if I did not shift my focus and find my grateful life, I would not come through. I would be lost—forever.

On the evening of July 4th, God shot a flare into the night sky, and I looked around my life with wide-opened eyes. I could see. And I began writing, trying to capture all of it before the light of the flare flickered and then disappeared into the ebony of night. It has truly been the most freeing experience of my life. And it turned out to be something of a life vest in my vast ocean of grief. I've held onto the fact that I could still find good in this world, despite the circumstances.

However, I arrived at documenting gratitude in the depths of sorrow is irrelevant, I suppose. I believe that every moment of my past perfectly prepared me to make the choice. My despair allowed me to surrender, to finally allow myself to connect to the magic that is all around us.

My journal entries were written at the end of the day each day. On some particularly trying days, I wrote the next morning.

I share my reflections with you because I believe we all are on the cusp of making that important connection in our lives. I share my very personal journey in the hopes that you can recognize that you too are resilient and see that there is always a way through. We have been conditioned to deny imperfection. But the truth is that life is messy and beautiful all at the same time. And you don't find joy only in the good times. You find it moment by moment—in the simple things. You find it one little thing at a time.

July 4th: Fireworks, Pace Cars, CD Mixes, and Rain

There are as many nights as days, and the one is just as long as the other in the year's course. Even a happy life cannot be without a measure of darkness, and the word "happy" would lose its meaning if it were not balanced by sadness.

~Carl Jung~

One little thing. What am I trying to do? Why do I feel I have to do it?

After *the* call, life changed. Forever. My son is missing. And I know what that means, even though we all continue to dance around the truth.

On this evening, I am thankful for the fireworks welcoming my son to heaven. I could not say those words aloud, for fear I would make something not yet confirmed true. I am thankful for my husband and his emotions. He cries, openly and freely weeping. He loves Stephen so. I am so grateful that I have a husband who can let his feelings show, who wears his heart on his sleeve and who loves my children so hard. I am thankful for him and understand that the only reason I have my footing right now is because he sits next to me.

I am thankful he knows better than to try and be the "man," treating me like a shrinking violet. When we ran to the car, his parents looked and asked him if it was wise for me to drive as I jumped into the seat. He simply said, "I am not going to tell her she can't drive." I needed to drive. I was a woman on a mission. I am grateful for the relationship we have together and how we are partners, equal halves.

I am thankful for the CD mix that Stephen left in my car, his favorite music, unknown and quirky artists, each song telling a story. It is funny, as Brady and I had such a long drive up here a few days earlier, but we did not even turn the stereo on. That's what I love about my relationship with Brady. We talked for the entire eight hours. We only turned it on when we were driving to Jordan Lake tonight. And it was primed and ready to go, almost as if Stephen had arranged it that way so we would know he was with us in the car. It was beautiful and soulful music, college music, rhythms that are only discovered in the years of transition between childhood and adulthood. That music, spoke to us as we drove through the night. It was as if it was guiding us to him.

I am so grateful for the feeling, the knowing that he was right there with us in the car. For one last time, I felt my sweet boy sitting in the back seat, as he had so many times before on happy trips or adventures. He was with us, hands on our shoulders, protecting us, making sure that we made it to the lake without harm.

Throughout the night, we were accompanied by what I labeled the "pace car." A small Toyota Camry, with California plates, that started driving in our direction in Kentucky. And, for a reason I will never understand, our pace car never left us until we were on the final road outside of Raleigh, taking the exit towards Jordan Lake. We would pass the car in the dark of night, and then, hours later, it would pass us. I never really got a good look at the driver or the occupants, but they drove with us, in the middle of the night, on lonely and unoccupied roads. And, each time we would pass each other, I would look at the California plate and smile. I would smile because I was getting a special message, one that was bigger than the simple things I knew and understood; one enveloped in the mystery of life and death. A message that confirmed that there is so much more than we can see or understand. The Camry had a vanity plate, which is not unusual in this ego-driven society we all live in. But it was what it spelled out.

"ONE LIFETIME"

To most, it would not have been significant, but for us?

The same words that were inked into Stephen's left flank. The tattoo on his left flank, a true rite of passage in his first weeks at NC State, an independent act taken based on his want and not my approval. I can't say I was happy about that tattoo at first. I was not. I was disappointed, I was in reality frustrated that he and his girlfriend had decided to do this without, what I thought, was much deliberation of the long-term consequences. But, with time, I realized he was a man, and he had made a choice based on what he wanted. Now, the fact that those two words were what he selected seemed rather poignant. With a beautiful apple, his tattoo read:

"ONE LIFETIME"

That pace car was no simple coincidence.

And finally, it was God. I had been asking Him some pretty tough questions as of late. I had not been impressed with Him and His lack of answers. But there He was. I could feel him, and the signal was loud and clear. He sat in the back of the Four Runner, with Stephen and Rudy, and on we drove through the night. I know it sounds crazy. I will never truly be able to articulate to anyone what the interior of the Four Runner was like for those 9 long hours. But we were not alone—of that I am sure.

July 5th: Conversations with God at the Shoreline

Deep, unspeakable suffering may well be called a baptism, regeneration, the initiation into a new state.

~George Eliot~

The back of an envelope that holds our cable bill. Sitting in the parking lot of the funeral home, I am scribbling on the back of an envelope my list of gratitude as I wait for the paramedics to bring my son's body back from the lake.

What am I doing? What is the one little thing that you can take goodness from on the day they recover your son's body? I can't believe I'm doing this, nor can I understand why I can't stop myself from doing it.

The Perfect Cove at Jordan Lake

As I walked down the trail, I could almost picture them the day before, galloping down this hill, with the anticipation of an outstanding 4th of July. I could picture his smile, as he ran ahead, looking over his shoulders at his friends. He was like that, running ahead, anxious to get to the "experience." On arriving, I paused, held my breath, and looked around, then collapsed with grief and pain. The dichotomous nature of life is quite something. This beautiful place was a paradise, and yet, the worst place on earth all at the same time.

The most beautiful location on earth. No one has a choice when it comes to death, but if you must go, this is a stunning place to be welcomed into heaven. The place of his death was almost like a glimpse into heaven itself. Looking around the serene cove, the water was still, motionless only except the few fish that would gently ripple the surface of the water with a turn of their tails. The trees were still, not a breath of air. The world was quiet, except for a few birds here and there, almost as if God had asked for a moment of silence out of respect. The lush, green trees reflected in the water and reminded me of my father's paintings from many years before. I loved it when he would paint the upside-down trees.

Realizing My Position in This

Sitting on the ground and negotiating with God was an education for me. For many years, I have been fortunate enough to be able to affect change on things in my life. I have found that when I set my mind to something, I can usually make it happen. But on this day, I realize that any sense of control I thought I had over my experiences was only an illusion. I see now that there is a power, a purpose, and a plan that is much bigger than me, so complex and intertwined I could never hope to understand it. And although that loss of power in the past would have stressed me tremendously, this time, it gives me some peace. I have been let in on a mystery. So, once I realized that my negotiation with God was not going to work, I surrendered. And the sounds that I uttered in that submission were ones of pain but also of peace as I let go.

My Maternal Connection

The special connection between mother and child is like no other; it is something that cannot be quantified, but it is there. It's a magical intuition, a knowing about the well-being of your baby, the knowing that comes from looking deep into their eyes in the quiet of a night feeding or the connection you feel when you comfort their hurts and know you are the only one that can do so. I've felt it when he was at school, and I would feel a sudden urge to call him only to find he was not having a good day. On this morning, as I looked over the lake, I knew right where he was. Rudy the Wonder Dog and I sat on the sand and looked toward the one specific spot in the water and asked God to bring him to us. Me and my brown dog, we just knew. And sure enough, that's where they found him. Knowing that as his mother, I was connected to him like that, even in death, made me thankful.

His Friends and Their Parents

There are certain times in life where the character of human beings becomes very apparent. This was one of those times. Too often in life, we are bombarded by what is wrong in this world. The nightly news will tell you about the masses who don't care, who only want to take or hurt. But the simple truth is, there is and always will be more good in this world than bad. I was reminded of that on this rainy morning. I was amazed by his friends, the people he surrounded himself with in his life. His choices in companionship did not disappoint me, they were everything a mother could hope for in her child's friends.

When we left the cove and drove over to the wharf where the search was being coordinated, we were met by them standing there, hearts on their sleeves, waiting for their friend. And with them, their parents, some strangers, who would not allow us to be alone in such a dark and painful time. I should not have been surprised really, looking at the kids they raised, a testament to their character. They stood with us, to be there to wait for the divers to find Stephen. They stayed at the shoreline with us during the most difficult moments of our life. On that day, his friends and their parents became part of our family. One mom in particular, she hugged just like my mom, with a tightness and intensity that made you feel for a moment that you were protected and would be okay. And for an instant, I did feel as if I had been sent one of my mom's hugs from heaven. And through it all, they did not look away. They stayed when others would have turned and left or not shown up at all. It was the greatest demonstration of compassion I have ever witnessed, a gift of kindness from people, some of them having never even met us prior to this morning. And in my darkness, I could still see those who held a candle for me so that I might see a flicker of light.

The Rescue Crew

They are the nameless, the ones that quietly go in and do the hardest job a human being could do. I know that. And after they brought my son to me, I hugged them all and told them, "Thank you for finding him so I could bring him home." It seems like a weird thing to be thankful for, but without them, I would have a life of uncertainty. Without them, I would have to walk away from that lake without my child, without saying goodbye.

Saying Goodbye

As difficult as it was to see him, I would not have changed a thing. I needed to say goodbye, to count my baby's fingers and toes, to have my last moments with his physical form in all its perfection. When Stephen was born, and his brother Matthew died, I was not given an opportunity to hold my baby and say goodbye. I do not harbor ill will for that; it was a different time, where the importance of this component of grieving was not yet understood. I am sure they thought I could not handle the experience. It is, to this day, one of the biggest regrets of my life. So, to be able to say goodbye, to be able to have the extremely sad moment that will be forever tattooed in my brain—it was a gift.

The Funeral Director

At the shoreline, Brady and I had discussed the need for an autopsy. Looking around at the cove and hearing the story from his friends, we had doubts about him struggling in the water. We found out he suffered a hard hit to the chest at hockey a few days earlier, had coughed up some blood, and had complained of a "pain in his heart" earlier that day. We felt, without a doubt, that this was related to his death. This serene cove, with his athleticism, should not have been an issue. But as the morning wore on, we realized to send him to UNC Chapel Hill to get an answer really would not give us peace or change the outcome in any way. In fact, it would simply prolong this experience, and we wanted to move to the point of the celebration of his life.

So, after weighing out the options, we made the decision not to request an autopsy and asked that he be brought to a funeral home. This was the best decision. The funeral director, a man who was local, operated the family-owned business with his wife. In his kindness, I could see his respect for us and our pain, for Stephen. It is rare these days, but once in a while, you meet someone who is living their purpose. Their job is not simply a profession but a passion, and every moment they are doing it, they are giving 110 percent. This was the man who comforted us on that day, comfort we would not have otherwise had if we had decided to push ahead to have definitive answers that would not have brought Stephen back to us.

My Husband

Brady carried me through this. Falling apart in his own right, he held himself together enough to be my one constant through that day. But it was not only the hugs, comfort, and love he gave me or how he quietly handled the arrangements, the phone calls, and the details I did not even notice. It was him and who he was every other day as well. You see, every time I looked at him, I could recall every moment of joy he had given to Stephen in the last 4 years of his life. He'd had a relationship with my boy that my plain words could never describe adequately. He had showed him unconditional love and acceptance and had taught him how to go after his dreams.

Brady was the personification of positive energy, and he showered Stephen with it, showing him how to grab life and get exactly what he wanted. I've often said that much like the lush foliage of the Carolinas, Stephen blossomed down here, and Brady was the fertilizer. And on this day, the first day of life without Stephen, I could not help but look at the man I married and know that Stephen had received a better ending because of him. I could not help but be grateful for that, as so many people die sad, angry, or alone. My child died happy, and we should all be so lucky to have people in our lives that help make that so in our last days.

My Family

I am blessed with the family I have. To say we are close would be an understatement. Our parents died in the early '90s, and we are one of the rare families that kept the glue. You often see siblings fall away from one another in the loss of their parents, but that did not happen with us. In fact, I believe in some ways, we became closer because of it. On that day, my family, although they were thousands of miles away, stood with me at the shoreline. I could feel them.

Priests and Prayers

We had driven all night and stood at the lake all morning. We had not slept in about 32 hours, and physically, we were exhausted. Everyone in Raleigh wanted us to stay, to rest. The kindness was overwhelming, and they all wanted to do something to alleviate some of our distress. But we wanted to just get home. And I wanted to talk to a priest. Reaching out to my church and God at that moment is something that I will always be grateful for in my life. I knew that I stood at a crossroads, and I had made a choice to choose the light.

So, for the worst day I have had in my entire existence, I did find things, little blessings to carry me through. Maybe they were not so little after all. Anything that could allow me to see the good in this day must be pretty special.

July 6th: Half-Awake Serenity, Long Lost Pictures, and One Cherished Email

What you leave behind is not what is engraved in stone monuments, but what is woven into the lives of others.

~Pericles~

At first glance, the only thing I could really be thankful for today was that split second between sleep and wakefulness. That moment at dawn when, for an instant, all of this was only a bad dream. For a brief instant, I felt peace, knowing I would see him downstairs, eating his banana and six to eight slices of toast with about a half a gallon of milk to drink. But alas, that was not to be true. That lingering feeling of dread in my stomach returned with the speed of wakefulness. I turned to my side and looked at the floor next to my bed and saw his weekend bag and knapsack from the lake. I stared at them for what seemed to be an eternity. I am not sure why I had brought them to my room, but I needed to be close to them. Perhaps it was because they were some of the last things he touched. Gazing on them, I had my first cry of the day. It is a funny feeling when you awake, and your eyelids feel puffy and large from crying yourself to sleep the night before. Then, you begin to cry again, and the new morning tears are almost cleansing, washing away the sleep and providing some relief, much like tea bags but far more convenient. I think I am thankful for the tears. They need to flow. I need to let them out, although the volume seems endless.

I shuffle downstairs, unable to lift my feet completely. Everything is so damn heavy. It hurts to blink. So, I start to look for pictures of him, to try and find some comfort. And oh, what treasures I find!

I find photos of him as a baby, so small and fragile; I never thought that he would grow to be so healthy, so vibrant and athletic. I could not see beyond the delicate little one staring at me with eyes of ebony. The eyes told me so much. Even at a day old, it seemed like he had experienced more life than I had. He was an old soul from the beginning.

Next, I found pictures of him as a toddler, with a huge smile and big eyes that would melt any heart—and the greatest pictures of him as a participant in my father's parades. On Sundays, we would have dinner as a family after Mass. My parents loved to have everyone together, and grandchildren were the single greatest joy to my parents. After we would push away from the table, stomachs full, Dad would take all of the grandchildren into his bedroom. You could hear them whispering, giggling, arguing, and planning. The bedroom door would swing open, and marching out the hallway was the most fantastic parade! Each participant with an instrument in hand, they were the most fanciful, world-renowned marching band known to man. Dad would be leading the charge, and the instruments ranged from a trombone or tin whistle to a covered cup full of split peas.

More than the pictures themselves, I am thankful for the memories, long forgotten recollections to remind me of all that we had. That is certainly a "one little thing" for today, a very tough day.

But there was so much more. As I prepared for the memorial and funeral in Newfoundland, Canada, I came across an email. I have no idea why I looked for it or how I found it. Rather, it was presented to me.

I will return to this email often in the future to remind myself of what we had, mother and child, showing me that taking the time to talk about the real stuff in life with the ones you love is more important than anything else you could prioritize. I am proud, as I read that email and others, that we were not satisfied to only have the mundane conversations in life because of apathy or fear of the truth. We talked at length about the life-changing things. We had the hard conversations. We spoke candidly about our own strengths and weaknesses. I am most proud of the fact I was not afraid to tell him of my stumbles or mistakes, and the lessons I learned. Somehow, I think it allowed him to see life for the imperfect miracle it was and let him feel safe enough to share his own experiences with me. Of all the relationships I have had in my life, the one I had with him was the most honest. Perhaps because he had been with me the longest and had walked the path right next to me, hand in hand. It is difficult to explain the peace I felt in my heart when I read the email exchange between us. The hurt eased, if only for a moment. I still ache but know the email is a gift, something that other mothers who experience this loss may not be as fortunate to find in their quest for comfort. I have, in writing, confirmation that all the lost moments and words I had been lamenting about were, in fact, said. And this email and others will serve as a reminder of all the other times that we had said "I love you" and "Thank you" and "You mean the world to me" and "I am proud of you" and on and on. I know that finding this email will be part of my healing and part of finding a purpose in all of this. Now, to be patient with God and Stephen and let them lead me to that peace . . .

After reading this email to my husband, we quietly cried together, thankful for the comfort of words of love spoken when it mattered.

Much to be appreciative for today.

From: Kelly Buckley

To: Stephen
Sent: Monday, April 20, 2009, 12:30 PM
Subject: RE: Life

Stephen,

I left you a phone message about this on Friday but wanted to write a little note. I agree with what you have said below. Talk to coach and let him know how you feel. As for hockey, I completely understand your feelings about your senior year and academics. You have invested a lot of yourself, and you want the team to do well. You are passionate and competitive. I will support you 100% whatever direction you decide to go in. But, whatever you decide, I know you will think it through, and it will be the best for you. Let's talk more about it when we see each other.

*As for what you are going to do with your life, that is a tough one. The transition from full time student to "all grown up" can be a little intimidating. For me, I was kind of limited to my choices based on my nursing profession. But I am still refining what it is **I WANT** to do with my life. I guess that is the important thing to remember. What you start off doing is and will be a stepping stone to the next place, until you find the right place for you.*

Once you finish with the pressures of exams, I want you to take some time this summer to really think about the type of life you want for yourself, knowing that you can do whatever you set your mind to.... you can. There are free aptitude tests online that could point you in the right direction, or at least suggest different options for you. I remember Brady telling me on the day of his graduation, he walked across the stage and did not have a clue what he would do with his life. But he had a great work ethic and a wonderful attitude, he was ambitious, and it all worked out. It will work out for you too. I know that all your buddies have this very direct path with their chosen engineering professions, much like I did with nursing. But believe me, someday about ten years from now, some may sit at their desk and wonder if they were too rigid when they made their choices. They may wish they had given themselves some flexibility.

The bottom line is this time next year you will be graduating with a great degree from a well-respected school. You are a very smart man, you are a strategic thinker, a great writer, a great athlete, you are logical (and believe me, there are less of you logical ones in the world than you might think), you are a giving and loving person, you are one of the hardest workers I know (along with Brady), and this will come for you.

As your mother, I am slightly biased, I realize that. But I've always seen the greatness in you. Now, whether that means you will be a great RCMP officer, or a great journalist (You are a fantastic writer), or a great Political Analyst, a teacher, or whatever . . .. you will bring greatness to it.

Sorry for being so longwinded with this, but I wanted you to know that I love you, support you, and believe in you.

Love you,

Mom

xoxoxo

From: Stephen

To: Kelly Buckley

Sent: Tuesday, April 21, 2009, 11:33 PM

Subject: RE: Life

Hi Mom,

Thanks for the words of wisdom . . . . . .

I will let coach know what's going on, and I will draft an email that thoroughly explains the situation, as I want to make sure that he understands where I am coming from. Right now, I am in the final push of the semester, but will draft one on the weekend or shortly after to let him know.

As for hockey I will keep thinking about it because I love hockey. We have an exciting schedule for next year, like midnight games in Kentucky, games against Maryland (D1), etc., but I hate to lose . . ..

I want more than anything to have some epiphany one day where everything is laid out for me and there is no more second-guessing or decisions to be made for my career path, but I can't force it, I guess. I will think about it more when I have free time . . .. .

I really appreciate all of the help you and Brady give me every day. If it wasn't for both of you I don't know what I would do. I am very lucky to have great parents like you who care for me and would do anything for me . . . . I really mean it. It doesn't matter what the situation is, no matter if it is my fault or if it is dumb luck, you both always seem to be there for me, and I can't thank you guys enough.

I love you very much, and I will call you tomorrow

Love,

-Stephen

July 8th: Gazebos, Gardens, and Butterflies Galore

What the caterpillar calls the end of the world, the master calls a butterfly.

~Richard Bach~

Okay, take a deep breath, because today is going to depend all on how you look at it. You can fall down and crumble up in a heap on the ground, or you can stare today in the face and give him the sendoff he deserves.

Brady and I dressed quietly in our black clothes. Black clothes and the sun of the Carolinas simply do not mix.

Where is this strength coming from? Maybe it was shock, maybe Stephen really was with us as we felt, giving us the courage to make it through this with grace. In any case, we kept moving and kept standing.

I knew I wanted to speak at his memorial, but I had no plan. Brady, on the other hand, had thought about what he wanted to say and was ready to go. I listened to him as he practiced in the car, wanting to have it just right for Stephen. Oh, how he loved him so. The love he had showered Stephen within the last years of his life will continue to be one of my little things of the day for years to come.

And then, the words came—and simply, as if I was transcribing them for Stephen. They flowed freely, and I knew what I would say to both celebrate the special human being he was and to comfort the young adults who quite likely were encountering one of their first experiences with death. Crafted on a yellow notepad in a moving vehicle, it was more than I wanted to say. I felt it was what Stephen wanted. It was as if I was speaking on his behalf. I cannot take credit no more than I can accept praise for the way that Stephen conducted himself while here on earth. And I wanted to, if only for a moment, speak to his friends about those special attributes rather than how he had been lost too soon. As I scribbled, I could see the faces of his friends at Jordan Lake that morning. I wanted to give them some comfort, something positive to take from this loss, *something*. I felt compelled to find the good. And calling it a compulsion seems like the most accurate explanation. I could not accept that this was it, that he was gone now, and it was time to move forward. I had to find something out of this that allowed his goodness to live on, even if only in remembrance.

His words, more than mine, were one little thing for the day.

I deliberately did not ask Brady or anyone else about what had been planned and what was in store for the day. I wanted to see him through the eyes of his friends, those whom he touched. I wanted to get a feel for the life he had built for himself, independent, starting the chapter of adulthood. I was not disappointed.

Arriving in Raleigh, we made our way to the gardens, where the service would be held. I could see his friends and hockey teammates beginning to gather, dressed in the same suits they probably wore on game day. I held the pain in my throat. It was a large and uncomfortable bulge in my neck, the aching only balanced by the gnawing feeling of utter despair in my stomach. Looking at them reminded me so much of Stephen—so much promise, enthusiasm, and confidence.

I paused, soaking up the surroundings. I needed to remember everything: the lush trees, the flowers, the beautiful and serene pathway leading to the Arboretum gardens where the service would be held. Everything reminded me of him with its simple splendor.

As Brady and I walked up the footpath, a beautiful, white butterfly fluttered alongside us. The erratic movement in his journey made him look as if he were trying to get our attention, to let us know he was our companion. Brady and I held hands, squeezing tightly to both hold each other upright and to give the other comfort.

It was the most picturesque place. Again, natural beauty much like the cove at Jordan Lake, peaceful and serene. I could have selected no better place to remember Stephen.

A white gazebo was the focal point of the event, with chairs all around. Pictures of Stephen were placed on a simple rock wall that encompassed the circular area. A banner with Stephen's portrait was hanging in the front, and to the left, they had his NC State Hockey Jersey. On top of the hanging stand was his helmet, strategically placed to look like the wearer was looking down in respectful reverence.

It was simple, it was stunning and beautiful, and it was so Stephen. I was thankful.

I was moved by the attendees. They came from far and wide, some flying in from all over the country to be here, to pay their respects to their teammate and friend. Professors, classmates, and friends came together to bear witness to a life that had touched them in some way or another.

I mulled around the crowd and greeted people, kind of in a fog really. Everything was calm, polite, and quiet. I smiled, shook hands, hugged, and tried to be gracious. Honestly, most of my morning was consumed with my thoughts of Stephen, looking around and having a private conversation with him.

And then, I noticed the butterfly. Flying around the gazebo, it came to a peaceful landing on the podium. I pointed to the little guy, sitting there for the longest while, as if it was readying to speak to the attendees. Butterflies. They were everywhere, flying all over the gardens. Dozens of them fluttered around, complementing this one magnificent white butterfly sitting at the podium.

As the service started, I listened to the kind minister speak to the group about the loss of someone so young. I continued to watch that lone butterfly, sticking by the podium. The wonder of it all. I remember thinking that I must cement this moment into memory. It was a wondrous thing. I needed that gift at that instant, and for that I will be thankful.

Following the minister, the "musketeers" approached the podium. The musketeers plus Marie. An eclectic group, these were some of the people he had spoken of most of when he had told Brady and I stories of his college life. Nathan, a quiet and old soul, we had the pleasure of having as a house guest just weeks prior. He was so kind, and as I looked at him, I was reminded of a conversation Stephen and I had about their friendship. Then there was C.J., who gregarious and funny, with a smile that I am sure got him out of a few tight spots with a simple flash of his pearly whites. There was Marie, once a girlfriend, then a friend, with a personality like sunshine and spring, a beautiful and tender soul and someone I wished could have had more time with the kind of attention and care only Stephen could give a person. And finally, there was Ross; I'd met him at the Hockey Arena, as he was the other goalie for the hockey team for Stephen's first year playing with NC State. It was an unlikely friendship, two goalies competing for game time, but they had bonded from the start.

As they each spoke, their words told me a story of a Stephen who was enjoying life to the fullest. Each one had a different twist, but they all talked about a person who was fun, who knew how to take care of people, and whom they loved as their friend. The butterfly responded to their words, fluttering and flying around their circle, pausing by each of them.

After they finished, many others got up to speak, and I was so comforted by the stories they shared about their "Canadian Steve." That's what they called him — or "Canadian," for short.

Brady spoke, and I was stirred by his loving words. I'm not sure how God works out things, but somehow, I feel that He made sure this man was by my side before it was time for Stephen to go. As I stood next to him, looking at him as he spoke, I knew that I was only standing because he was holding me up.

It felt good to talk to his friends. My voice only caught once in my throat. It was at the point in my words where I wanted to tell the group that *"I choose happiness"* and I wanted them to do the same. Those three words stuck for a minute, and I had to make the determined effort to push them out of my mouth. I knew that was what I wanted, what Stephen wanted, but I just wasn't sure if it would ever materialize. As much as I knew in my heart I must speak those words, I will be honest in this record and admit I wonder if happiness will ever be synonymous with my life again.

In 3 short years at NC State, Stephen had built a terrific life for himself. Brady and I could feel his energy with every conversation he had with us about the future. He was happy, and today, as I looked around, I could see why. I could see the kind of people he associated with, and I could see that he had touched them. I could appreciate, even though he was only 23, how he had affected people. Perhaps his happiness was not with anticipation of the future but rather due to the unconscious awareness that he had achieved his purpose. He was at the pinnacle of his life; he was living a life to the fullest, with joy. Isn't that what we all should aspire to do, no matter how much time we have on our own clocks?

I was humbled by this day, by the memorial, by the reception afterwards. I was thankful for the friends, the teammates, and the character of the human beings that he shared his life with.

Later, waiting in the airport, Brady and I would take a moment to view the DVD of the service. We knew the day was magical, and we had felt his spirit with us. But as we watched the DVD, butterflies flew across the screen in the most amazing display.

As I said at the beginning, this day would be what I chose to make of it. I choose happiness. I choose magic and mystery and butterflies. I choose love. I am grateful, no matter how hard it is for me to say it.

July 9th: Going Irish on the Flight Attendant

Compassion automatically invites you to relate with people because you no longer regard people as a drain on your energy.

~Chögyam Trungpa~

The gratitude between our travel days seems to merge them together, so my recording of these days is not clean and separate. Much like life, things bleed into other things. My thoughts are mixed up, much like my emotions. I am on a roller coaster, with feelings of extreme sadness combined with gratefulness that I do not quite understand.

I am sitting at the gate and waiting for the flight, with Stephen sitting on our lap. It seems funny to type that, but Brady and I placed that bag between us much like a new mother would hold and dote on her newborn. We encountered many, in security or on the flight itself, who approached, to either move or examine that bag, only to quickly realize that was not an option to be entertained. Perhaps it was my eyebrow, or the intensity of how I or Brady clutched on to the bag. In any case, most of our travels were uneventful.

Boarding the flight for the last leg of the trip, I was anxious and exhausted. It was now midnight, and we had been up since well before 6 a.m. the day before. I just wanted to bring him home. Stepping onto the aircraft, I managed a weak smile toward the flight attendants who were assisting with boarding. They did not smile back. In my observations of people since July 4th, I noticed how kindness changed how people reacted to you. I was giving it a try. It did not work.

One flight attendant in particular appeared to have no joy and was focused on her own story. It was obvious that she was tired, and she was not happy about being on this late-night flight to Newfoundland, a place in the middle of the North Atlantic. Her scarf was slightly skewed to the left, her makeup was not as fresh as it had been at the beginning of her shift, and her hair was beginning to fall from the updo. Had I had more on reserve, I would have smiled more brightly, but instead I quietly made my way to my seat. Brady and I settled ourselves for the flight and placed Stephen between the two of us.

As the flight readied to take off, this same frustrated, dissatisfied flight attendant made her way down the aisle. As she made her first pass, I watched her talk with someone a few rows ahead of us. As she shook her head, her body language was, well, not inviting. She needed a day off. When she passed by us, she looked at the bag between the two of us. She paused and walked on. The desk clerk had indicated she would let the flight crew know we were traveling for bereavement reasons, and I had just hoped she would choose not to address this. But she did.

"You are going to need to put that bag under your seat."

The written word cannot convey the tone adequately, but it was a mixture of condescension and just pure frustration that we were not clever enough to know this in the first place. My words caught in my throat, and Brady was trying to speak before me to spare me the hurt of having this conversation. But he was also trying to help this lady, even if she did not necessarily deserve the assistance. Brady knew me. He knew what my razor-sharp response would be. We had joked in the past when we would have heated and passionate discussions. He would look at me and say, "Don't go all Irish on me." Both proud of our Irish roots, this was a running joke.

Before Brady could respond, she pointed her manicured finger and said again, "You need to put *that* under your seat." There was no smile, not a hint of kindness; you could feel her unhappiness oozing off her body like a heavy, overwhelming scent of cheap perfume.

"I can't put *this* under the seat. I am sorry." I said.

"You are required to put *this* under your seat," she barked back.

"I am sorry, *this* is *my son*, and I will not be putting him under the seat." I replied, the tone of my voice escalating an octave with every syllable. In the corner of my eye, I caught a glimpse of Brady's face. Priceless.

I thought those words would be strong enough, poignant enough to make her back down and get her the hell away from us for the rest of the flight. They did not.

"I know what *it* is, but *it* still needs to go under the seat. Do you know I could get fined?"

WOW.

Double WOW.

Did she actually say that? Did she really actually say that? I thought. Did she honestly think I cared if she was fined? "It" needs to go under the seat???

For an instant, I pictured the news headline about the grieving woman being escorted from the flight next to a photo of none other than myself with clumps of blond hair in both of my clenched fists.

"I'm sorry; my son will *not* be going under this seat." I said once again, making eye contact with her so she could read between the lines of the simple words.

"Okay, well I guess you can keep *it* there. But I hope you know; I could get in trouble for this. I could get fined if someone found out." And with that, she walked away, moving on to the next inconvenient traveler who was put on this flight to make her evening uncomfortable. And as she moved her way down the aisle, I listened to her conversations. She was in fact unhappy with everything. It was not just us but everything.

So, why is this event recorded in my journal of gratitude? A couple of reasons. I believe those people that come into your life and create friction are your biggest instructors. Not your favorite teachers, but the ones who will give you lessons worthy of remembrance. This abrasive and unhappy lady showed me how destructive and hurtful selfishness can be, how much you miss in the care of others when you are self-consumed and focused only on your own story.

And second, I am grateful for this lady because she was a spotlight. Her actions did not diminish or hurt me, but rather illuminated further the depth of the kindness of all the others who had crossed our path on this night, or since the 4th of July.

Needless to say, Stephen sat between us for the entire flight. Brady and I held hands and touched the bag, keeping Stephen close. And, when we landed in St. John's, I exhaled. I flashed my pearly whites at that flight attendant when I walked off the plane. "Hope you have a great night. Thanks so much!"

Let's hope that maybe I was one of her teachers that night as well.

Driving from the airport, a thick layer of early morning mist lay low over the water in the multitude of ponds that we passed. The landscape was rough, with rocks, trees, and moss mixing to become terrain that was both brutal and breathtaking all at the same time. And, as if God had wanted to give us a coming attraction, every so often the tree line would break to reveal an unobstructed view of the Atlantic Ocean with the sun rising over the horizon. I love where I live, and North Carolina is the prettiest of places. But there was something about this place. The beauty was not manicured but was the untouched version of magnificence from God, unaltered from His original vision. It was cleaner and seemed more real to me. I am sure it is how everyone feels when they return home. I was grateful.

Yes, Stephen, we were home. We were home to the place that we had longed for since the moment we had left so many years before. We were home, in the place where people knew us and loved us, a place with our history.

July 10th: The Rock—Where It Is Cold, but the People Keep You Warm

Call it a clan, call it a network, call it a tribe, call it a family.
Whatever you call it, whoever you are, you need one.

~Jane Howard~

We are home, back on "The Rock," a title Newfoundlanders use when describing our province. I feel surrounded by the love of my family. That is a big thing I am thankful for today. It will always be home to me, no matter where I live or how much time lapses between my visits. I am so proud I grew up here, and believe my roots are the reason for most of my strength.

About 10 years before, I climbed into a cab in Edmonton, Alberta, on my way to some meeting. The cab driver struck up a conversation with me and instantly recognized the hint of a Newfoundland accent in my voice. "You're a Newfie?" he asked and laughed a rich laugh, peppered with a throaty character that could only come from smoking way too many cigarettes.

I braced myself. I had found that living in the West, being asked if you were a Newfie usually preceded a joke from someone about Newfoundlanders. Oh yes, if you were born in Newfoundland, you know all of them and became accustomed to being a punch line from time to time.

But instead, he said, "You know, I've traveled all over this country, and I loved Newfoundland when I was there about 20 years ago. I tell people that yes, Newfoundland is cold, but the people keep you warm."

It was the nicest thing that anyone has ever said to me about Newfoundland, especially since moving away some years before that. And his statement was so, so true. I smiled and could feel those "people" keeping me warm already. One little thing.

Today, we were having a celebration of life for Stephen. My family planned everything. It was so strange for me to simply step back and let things just happen. I had spent my life working to ensure I was in control of my circumstances. To relinquish the need for power was liberating.

And once again, putting my faith in others did not disappoint me, for the room was covered with so many beautiful pictures of Stephen from all stages of his growth. A slideshow with photos of Stephen's life was played. There was music and so many people. It was personal, it was simple, and it was him.

As I moved from person to person, I noticed that in between those quiet conversations, people wandered the perimeter, perusing the pictures, seeing his life. Most of the people in this room had not seen Stephen for years, since he was a child, maybe 10 or 11. So, for many, the pictures around the room told a story of how he lived, the adventures he'd had within those short years. I was thankful, so very appreciative for those pictures, because Stephen had lived. He had lived a life so rich and full, and I wanted others to see and to recognize that. Looking around at the moments captured in Stephen's lifetime, I was thankful for the adventures and for the good times. The images not only served as a remembrance today but as a reminder to me. He had lived a full life here on earth. He had lived. There was a lot to be thankful for as I looked around. Even with Brendan, as difficult as it was for him to be here, I was glad that he had an opportunity to experience it. I wished he had been able to be with us in North Carolina as well. It was important, although painful, to see the tribute to someone's life, the passage between life and death. I had always thought it was a mistake to completely hide that reality from children. I believe that we should choose to show them, to help them in their understanding that it is as much a part of life as birthday parties and summer vacations. I did not want my child to hurt, but I also understood that through his wounds he would gain wisdom, just as I did. As his mother, I had an immense and solemn responsibility: to ensure that he, much like the choices I was now making, would also choose to learn from this instead of becoming bitter, to take the good from life and not to focus on the bad. I am both thankful and daunted by the task at the same time.

There were so many stories. His friend Katie told me that when they would go ice skating, Stephen was one of her only friends that she would allow to push her wheelchair around the ice. And he would act silly and dance around the chair and sing. I remembered the weekly school skating sessions. Stephen did love to skate, and that was years before he had even started to play ice hockey.

But I had no idea that he had done that. I had no clue that he had been such a good friend. It meant so much to me to hear that. It meant so much that after 15 years had passed, that Katie would take the time to come out today and tell me that story.

And, my niece's husband, whom I had not even realized had shared an experience with Stephen, told me a wonderful story as well. He talked about coaching Stephen in baseball. It had been a crucial game in the season, and Stephen had been up at bat. They had players on base, and if they won this game, it would mean advancing closer to the finals for the season. Stephen had made the hit and was running the bases. But the runner ahead of him took a nasty fall and was tagged out.

He said, "Stephen could have run past him, and if he had, we probably would have won the game and moved on, closer to the championship. But he didn't. He stopped to help his friend and teammate instead. He was tagged out, and they lost the game."

I could not believe it. As I sat quietly later in the day, I thought about Stephen's competitive nature and how he loved to win. But in the analysis of his life, I've found some interesting facts. His favorite game of hockey that he ever played was, in fact, a loss. The baseball game, because of his kindness, was a loss as well.

I am so, so grateful today, because through his death, I am learning that my son knew the real meaning of winning in life.

July 11th: My BFF, the Christian Brother, the iPod, and the Funeral

Participate joyfully in the sorrows of the world. We cannot cure the world of sorrows, but we can choose to live in joy.

~Joseph Campbell~

Staring at the ceiling and contemplating my existence. It's starting to become a habit. It is actually a good thing. Before Stephen's death, I recognize that I was, like so many others, on autopilot in many aspects of my life. Contemplative or meditative thinking was simply not a priority listed for the day in my planner. There was always a task or a chore or a distraction that would prevent that quiet time to reflect and ponder. That has now changed, and for that I am grateful.

I need to prepare myself. Today is Stephen's funeral, the day we bury Stephen's physical remains next to his brother Matthew. As the sun sets on this day, we close this chapter and begin the journey of discovering and learning about our life without him with us physically. It is difficult, having never, ever thought that I would have to consider how I would carry on and live without another child.

But as much as I did not think I would be in this place, here I sit. And I must continue to live.

Life: your heart is full at one moment and broken at the next.

And now, it was here. In just a few short hours, we would be saying our final farewells.

Preparing for the Mass silently, I looked over the words I intended to speak. A variation of the words articulated at the Raleigh, North Carolina, memorial, I again knew that they were not my own. In my solitude, I reached into my purse and pulled out Stephen's iPod. I had been unable to get it to work up to this point, but on the first try this morning, the screen lit up, and it was ready to go.

Tentatively, I looked at the playlists, the music. I clicked on the playlist titled "Marie." A soft melody played in my ear, and I began to cry. Brady, with his hands on my shoulders, comforted me as I quietly wept. I could feel Stephen with us. I could feel his spirit all around us as we sat there, much in the same way as we had the night we had driven to the lake. I gave Brady an ear bud, and we sat, listening quietly, weeping tears that were mixed with both deep, unending sorrow and an appreciation for what we had shared with Stephen. I was so thankful for that quiet moment with him, prior to the funeral Mass.

My oldest and dearest friend Tracey came to see me before going to the church. Tracey had been a constant since the evening of July 4th and for the 23 years before that night as well. We had been best friends since the sixth grade.

Our friendship had grown over the many years of our lives. We had been through challenges and triumphs, hills and valleys, times when we thought we had it all figured out and times when we realized we knew nothing. Our relationship is deeper these days, richer from the life journeys we have shared, from the perspectives we have gained in our transitions from being someone's child to someone's parent. We have history. And if you are lucky enough to have a friend who has that much history with you and loves you just the same, you are blessed. Our bond has stood the test of time, of differences, of disagreements, and of life directions. It has endured like a river rock that becomes smoother and more beautiful from the years of water rushing over it but remains just the same.

Tracey was Stephen's godmother, having stood beside me so many years before as we had blessed the beginning of Stephen's life. Looking back at the pictures of his Baptism Day, it is laughable — not only for the Flock of Seagulls '80s-style haircuts and the eyeglasses as big as dinner plates but for the absurdity of the situation, as we thought we were mature and grown up. As the pictures clearly indicate, we were children. It looked like a school play rather than a passage of life.

From that moment, she had loved Stephen with an intensity that was beautiful to see.

And she stood here today with me much like she had for so many years before. So, I sat her down and gave her an ear bud. As she listened, she cried, as I did. It was like one final, deep dialogue with Stephen.

At the church, I held Brendan's hand until it was time to speak.

And then it was time. My words were not elegant, but it felt good to tell those who loved him that because of his choices, he had lived a full life.

Conversations with Stephen: The Wisdom of a Child

First, I want to begin by thanking all of you for supporting and loving us and celebrating the life of Stephen. It has been such a source of comfort for our family to read and hear how he touched the lives of so many.

I, like so many of you, have been trying to find purpose and peace with all of this. I know the best way to honor Stephen is to continue to celebrate life as he did every day.

While looking for photos, I found an email exchange between Stephen and me from a few months back. Talking about hockey and life (those conversations always went together and were more closely related than you might think), we told each other what mattered. We talked about what we wanted from life, how much we had to appreciate, how we were so lucky to have this amazing family that loved without condition. As I read our words, I suddenly had peace in a raging sea of emotion. I realized that all of the important things had, in fact, been said. So, as a fitting tribute to my beautiful boy, I wanted to share some of the things we talked about in his lifetime. To be honest, not all of the insight came from the parent but rather from this gentle and patient soul we remember today.

1. As Stephen did, LIVE IT. Jump out of bed every morning and live the life God gave you . . .. . to the fullest. Take chances, climb trees, don't put off your goals. Don't postpone happiness. Just choose to be happy. Don't say you'll get it on the way back. Stop now, smell the roses, eat the ice cream, take the picture.

2. Wear your rose-colored glasses. EVERY DAY. See the silver lining. Laugh more, the out-loud belly laughs, snorts and all. Find the good in every person and situation, EVEN THIS ONE. Don't judge others. Accept differences and understand everyone has a distinct role in this dance called life.

3. Be present in your life. The here and now. Don't hold yourself back because of yesterday. Don't tie yourself down with strings of fear because of the uncertainty of tomorrow. Don't miss the now, even a painful now like today. Drink it up, learn from it, and see what it makes for your tomorrow.

4. Bring excellence to what you do. On the ice, Stephen would skate out to the crease, tap both posts with his stick, and it was "game on." He gave everything, 100 percent of the time. He loved the spirit of competition. But his true excellence was most visible off the ice: how he loved his family, adored his little brother, nurtured friends in need, lived in the moment, and lifted people up.

5. Finally, don't let things go unsaid. Give love freely, even to those who are not easy to love. Say "I love you" and "Thank you" as much as you brush your teeth. Wear your heart on your sleeve and know that there can never be regret by doing so . . ..

Stephen would not want us to measure his life in years. Rather, I think he would prefer we measured his age by the amount of kindness he showed to others, the hours he listened and advised, the loads he lifted and carried for family and friends, the number of smiles, the number of people he loved without condition or agenda, or expectation for anything in return. If we measured those things, it would appear he died an old man, life rich and full, purpose on earth achieved.

As my husband and I drove through the night to reach Jordan Lake, I watched community fireworks light up the night sky in celebration of the 4th of July. I could not help but think, for this year, they were welcoming an incredibly special new addition to heaven . . .. where . . ..

The ice is always smooth, the refs are good, he's starting every game, and his team is ready. And his worthy opponent will make him stand on his head before the third period ends with him victorious. Just as he loved it.

We could all choose to close our hearts at a time like this, be angry and bitter or confused. I stood at that fork in the road of my life in the last hours of July 4th, 2009. AND I CHOOSE HAPPINESS. I choose it, and I want you to do the same.

In that email, I told him I, although a tad biased, thought he was destined for greatness, on a path to change things and people for the better. Please help me make that true by honoring his spirit and living your life with the kind of joy he had.

Walking back to the pew, my heart felt light, no matter what the hurt. I was glad I did it, and I was pleased that I had been allowed to have this personal moment.

Following the completion of the Mass, people gathered on the church steps. I looked around, taking in the scene. When I was a teenager, I had stood on these steps after Mass, hoping to get a glance from a boy I had liked. I had walked out on these steps, releasing the held-in emotions following the funeral of my mother, then my father. I had stood on these same steps on my wedding day, with Stephen by my side. Today, I looked around and saw love, not pain. And standing, assisted with his cane, was Brother Slattery. Things had officially come full circle.

Brother Slattery had been one of my teachers at St. Michael's High School, but he had taught me so much more than the curriculum listed in the school agenda. Deep as the ocean, he made you ponder the important things in your life, and he had come to me in a time when I needed some pondering. I remember one particular day, he had been frustrated with someone's lack of performance in his class, and he had said, "You go through your life, and you don't pay attention. You don't pay attention in my class, nor do you do so in your life. I bet you cannot even tell me how many stairs lead up to the senior side of this school. You walk them every day, and you do not even know the answer."

He had this slow, cold, molasses-like drawl that had always left me with a feeling of anticipation for the next word.

I thought about that statement, and some 24 years later, I can still recite it. That day, I did not know the answer to the question about the stairs. But from that moment on, I counted every stair of every staircase my feet would touch. And I paid better attention to a few other details of life as well.

When I left school in the spring of '86 to have a baby, I was very unsure of where I would go from that point in my life. After giving birth to Stephen and losing Matthew, I was farther from answers than before. My summer was a blur of lifestyle adjustments, pressure, diapers, feedings, and feelings of deep anxiety and inadequacy in my ability to succeed at anything. The last thing on my mind was school, and to be honest, I did not know if I could face people. One quiet summer afternoon, the mail arrived, and in the pile sat a letter for me with the school letterhead prominently displayed. I paused and looked at it for a long time, thinking what was written inside would have to be something undesirable. Although I was a good student academically, I somehow had instantly convinced myself this must be related to the fact I was not worthy of returning. But instead of the correspondence of doom, it was a simple handwritten letter from Brother Slattery. In it, he told me that life's challenges sometimes turn out to be good teachers and that God has a plan. He said I was smart and that I needed to come back to school and finish and do good things in my life. That letter gave me the courage I needed to return after summer break, to go on and have a successful senior year, to believe I could be the Class Co-President or the Valedictorian. He never knew, nor did anyone else, but I read that letter thousands of times, urging myself to believe him.

And there he was, standing there with assistance, having traveled more than 5 hours from his retirement home to be here. I have to say, God has it all figured out. He knew what I needed today, and somehow, He had given it to me. For when I saw that sweet man's face, the feelings flooded me, filled my heart. I was not alone. I was surrounded by love.

The post-funeral gathering turned into a traditional Irish wake. It was personal, it was funny. We listened to Stephen's iPod mix, and each song told my family the story of him. It brought out feelings in people that otherwise would not have been expressed. It turned a very hard day into a celebration of gratitude. And do you know the most amazing thing? For a great part of the day, we were listening to the playlist called "The Lake." I tell you, that is resilience, baby.

It was a gift. It taught us that grief does not need to be mournful. It hurts, but it can be a celebration of a life worth honoring. Later that day, the cousins all stood on the front lawn, posing for pictures, with Brendan holding Stephen's picture proudly. They acted silly, posing in the most ridiculous fashion, flexing their biceps, and sticking out their tongues at the camera. All of them were there together, on the lawn, clutching the picture of the one lost from the group. The *Resilient Russell Family*—that is my clan.

I found so many things to be thankful for on this day, much more than I thought possible. I believe Stephen would have been proud of us all, finding the good in the worst of situations. Thank you for a day that he deserved.

July 12th: Home, Butterflies, Playlists, and Weeping at the Cemetery

What you leave behind is not what is engraved in stone monuments, but what is woven into the lives of others.

~Pericles~

Well, all is complete.

Memorial in North Carolina. Check.

Memorial and celebration of child's life in Newfoundland. Check.

Funeral. Check.

As I lie in bed this morning, the finality of the whole thing begins to sink in, to seep into my skin like an expensive, wrinkle-resistant, Vitamin-infused moisturizer I spent far too much money on in the hopes of cheating the destiny of aging. It is funny how the frivolous and extravagant things that I both have enjoyed and sought after at times in my life seem very trivial and unimportant these days. My life has been stripped bare and looks nothing like it used to. But I am not sure if that is a bad thing necessarily. I actually think, despite how I got here, that my new simplified view of life here on earth is a good thing.

As I get up, I can hear the multitudes in my sister's house, talking and starting the day, everyone sitting together and having coffee. They love me so much. I know it and I feel it, but I am not ready to be part of their conversation yet. I explain this to my husband, and with iPod in hand, my dark glasses and baseball hat, I set off to be alone with my thoughts. Returning to your hometown is an emotional experience in the easiest of times. Coming back to your roots forces you to look at those roots and see where they are both strong and weak, healthy and diseased. I've always found that each time I come home, I remember certain things about my youth that I am now old enough to process from a different perspective. Not that I had a traumatic childhood—I did not. At least not at the hands of others. I was surrounded by love. It's just funny how time away gives you a new viewpoint on things that seemed wholly insurmountable so many years ago.

I take a familiar route, one that I used to stroll to get to my elementary school. Walking these very same streets as I did as a child, my thoughts are flooded with memories, both of my own youth and of my early beginnings as a young mother with Stephen.

I would walk this path, rain or shine, usually accompanied by my neighbor Mike on our way to Notre Dame Academy. It was a wonderful school, connected to a convent and right next to the cathedral. The old school is long gone now, torn down a number of years ago, but the school song still lingers in my memory.

"Deo duce" let our hearts echo—

That's the key to victory day by day.

All hail to thee, our cherished alma mater,

Notre Dame, the star to light the way.

It was only 5 years ago that I looked up the definition of *Deo duce* and found it to mean *with God for a leader*. I like that.

I smile as I walk by a house on the route, remembering one early spring afternoon when I was in fifth grade. I was "dillydallying," as my mother called it, and it was taking me an extra-long time to make it home from school. The sun was shining, the snow was finally starting to melt, and I was in no rush. As I passed the house in question, there sitting in the melting snowbank was a 10-dollar bill. I was so thrilled and quickly ran the rest of the way home to tell my mother, wet 10-dollar bill held between my soggy mittens and flapping in the wind.

And then the bottom fell out of my excitement.

"Do you think that it might belong to the people who live in that house?" my mother had asked.

I had already had the money spent in my mind.

"Wait until your father gets home, and we can ask him," she said.

To this day, I think she knew what he would say, but he wanted to make me think a little about the fact that the money had originally belonged to another person.

When Dad came home that evening, he informed me, "I think we need to put it on the radio and see if anyone claims it as their own. If no one claims it in 24 hours, the money is yours." And then, in Dad fashion, he took the 10-dollar bill, still wet from the snow, and placed it on top of the radio we had in the kitchen. "Now, come back tomorrow, and if it is still there, it is yours to spend."

I can't help but smile at the memory, even though my mind is clouded with so much emotion. As I round the corner, a lone butterfly flits and flutters around me, following me for a bit down the road. Butterflies. They have been a constant companion since Stephen's death.

As I look at the butterfly walking down the road with me, I am flooded with more memories. I am 16 years old with a newborn baby. I am walking down this very road with Stephen in the stroller, self-conscious and worried about the looks of those passing me, knowing I was too young to be a mother. Too young but a mother indeed. Oh, what a beginning he and I had! I carried that feeling with me for many years in his life, feeling less than adequate in my role because of my age. It truly has been only in the last five years that I could see how rare and special our relationship truly was, and one of the biggest reasons was how we had started. How freeing it had been to let go of all those hang-ups and simply love each other. How healing to see the wonder of it all finally. Life is funny. As I think back on that, it seems like a lifetime ago, but at the same time, it feels as if it was only yesterday.

I stroll by the Knights of Columbus building. I call it that, although it has been sold and has not served that function for some years now. My father was a Grand Knight here at one time. Every year, they had a huge softball tournament, and my father would draw cartoon character players for each one of the players. In the large hall upstairs, I as a little girl would not only color and cut out those softball players but help hang them all over the walls in anticipation of the out-of-town team's arrival. At the end of that tournament, I watched, as I grew, those players look around for their "character" to take home. My father had personalized each one, with their number and hair color and even their body shape. My father had no idea of his talent or how much he touched other people. To this day, his wondrous and huge spirit still awes me. I am blessed, you know, even if I can't quite feel it just yet. I know it in my heart. I came from a family of wonder and giggles, of adventures and love, where special days were really special, where we went the extra mile for one another, where we handled adversity with grace and dignity. I had a son who absorbed every bit of that and carried it with him throughout all of our travels, all of our ups and downs.

As I continue the walk, I pass by the mill, now a vacant and sad reminder of a busier time for our town. The mill closed earlier this year, and the town appeared to still be adjusting to the loss and trying to find its new identity without something that had played an enormous part in the entire purpose of the community. I could relate, as I was on a similar journey, although more personal. My father had worked in that mill for his entire career. He performed back-breaking work for long hours to support and take care of his family.

The butterfly, who had left me alone with my thoughts for a while, returned with me on my travels. I was thankful for sunglasses, because the waterworks were flowing freely by this point in the journey. Mr. Butterfly stayed with me for most of the remaining walk, as if he knew I needed the support to make it to the cemetery. Arriving there, I made my way to Stephen's grave.

The temporary white cross stood like a soldier on guard. I sat quietly next to it and looked at the two graves, he and Matthew, side by side once more. Tears flowed freely and were followed by deep and anguished sobs. As had been the case so many times in the past week, I could only say his name. I miss him so, so much. How can I go on without him? As the tears subsided, I listened quietly to the music in my ears, feeling hollow. And then, as if to serve as another reminder of the fact that there is a bigger design and I am not alone, my butterfly returned. It fluttered around the graves of my family, my parents. It pitched and stayed.

I am thankful. I am thankful because as deep as the wound is, I have faith that it will heal. I have surrendered, and I've decided to put my faith in God and a bigger plan. I can look back over my life and see how divine intervention has played a part in getting me where I needed to be, to bringing people into my life that would forever change the direction it would take. I am thankful for the gifts of Stephen and Matthew. I am forever transformed for the better because of their impact on me.

Heading back to the house, I can smile. For although the physical remains of my two children are together in the cemetery, they both rest gently in my heart and will be part of my life in the days and years to come. I will see them in the random acts of kindness I show to others. I will see them in the people I love without condition or expectation. I will see them in the paths I choose to take going forward. I will honor them both and will show my thanks for my time with them.

July 17th: Friends and Family Who Love Me . . .

Home is not where you live, but where they understand you.

~Christian Morgenstern~

Well, this is the last day. The last day in Newfoundland. As I lay awake in bed this morning, I can't help but feel a slight sense of dread for the travel portion of this event coming to an end, not only because of the great comfort of family but because I know that when the flight touches down in Raleigh tomorrow, we are back to reality. When we walk out of the airport, we begin the next part of our journey. And I could pretend that I am ready for it. But I am not. I am scared, frightened like a child, and I am not sure if I can do it.

But today, I will be thankful, grateful that I am surrounded by family who loves me and knowing that they will only be a phone call away. I am blessed with friendships that have lasted my lifetime and continue to bloom with each passing year. I am thankful for the healing elixir I have sipped for the past number of days in my homeland. It is a mixture of love and unwavering support, and I hope it will get me through the coming weeks.

July 18th: The Miracle of an Uneventful Flight, Neighbors, Pajamas, and Home

Joy and sorrow are inseparable. Together they come, and when one sits alone with you at your board, remember that the other is asleep upon your bed.

~Kahlil Gibran~

The plane touches down. I look out the window and see the heat, hanging in the trees. I can't quite describe it adequately, but it was something I noticed when I first moved to the South. You can see the heat—or at least this North Atlantic girl can.

It is curious how you can be so hurt that you feel like a spectator in your own emotions. I suppose it is a protectionist tactic of the brain, to disconnect you so you can survive and get through the worst of it. You see so much more this way.

Back at the car, I take a deep breath. Home. As we begin to drive, I quietly weep. Thank God for the sunglasses. Yes, I suppose if I am committed to this gratitude thing, I will say thank you for the sunglasses. They have covered my eyes from the blazing sun, from the curious looks of people passing by as I openly bawl. They have covered the Samsonite baggage that sits below my eyes, and they shield my eyes now as I weep.

I don't want to be here. This reality is too painful. We continue to drive, and we are all kind of quiet. No words are spoken, but I know we are all feeling the same. We drive past the exit for Jordan Lake. I sob. Yes, it is all still happening. It is all still very real. As we zoom past the exit, I think about that morning, and I cry some more. I am broken, and I don't know if I can be fixed. I don't know if I want to be fixed.

This does not sound very thankful, does it? Let's regroup.

I am thankful for the sunglasses, as I said.

I am thankful for arriving home and seeing the enthusiastic and somewhat desperate greeting from Rudy the Wonder Dog. He missed us so, and I know he is hurting too. I am glad that we are all back together.

I am thankful for the love. Our neighbors—with food, cards, and support—have eased our pain. I tell you, if people truly understood what should be valued in this world, they would determine property values by the character and kindness of the people living in them. And we would proudly be able to say that we live in the most affluent neighborhood in the country. I am thankful.

I am thankful for my pajamas, my bathtub, and my bed. I am thankful for the exhausted cuddle that I had with Brendan this evening. I am not sure who needed it more. I am thankful for Stephen's bags, still sitting on the floor by my bed. I missed looking at them. And yes, I know at some point I have to move them, to unpack them. But not yet. For now, I am thankful I have them and can look at them and be close to his spirit.

So, the list is simple, but we are still grateful. The day was rough, no doubt about it, but we made it. And life will go on, not in the same way as before, but it will continue, nonetheless. With my baby in my heart, my two other boys at my side, and Rudy the Wonder Dog, we will survive.

July 19th: The Scent, the Wallet, and the Condom

There are stars whose light only reaches the earth long after they have fallen apart. There are people whose remembrance gives light in this world, long after they have passed away. This light shines in our darkest nights on the road we must follow.

~The Talmud~

We are home, back to our routines. But nothing seems normal. Nothing in this life seems quite the same. In fact, when I do get a flash of the familiar, it really hurts. I mean real, tremendous pain. It causes me to stop in my tracks, to feel a tightening in my throat, a constriction in my windpipe, and a loss of breath for a moment. And slowly, the clock starts again, and I begin to move forward. These moments of agony come quickly and without warning, lacking in rhyme or reason. I can be brought to my knees by a meaningful memory or by something that appears to be unrelated to Stephen in any way, shape, or form.

I am thankful for the hurt. I know it sounds strange, but I am thankful for the pain, as it is my teacher. I am thankful for the moments when I lose my breath, because it gives me gratitude for the moments I breathe easy or laugh with my son or my husband. I ache, but I am facing the pain and the truth.

The bags still sit by the bed. Brendan gallops into the room and picks up one of the knapsacks that have served as a shrine for some weeks now. He immediately opens it and starts eyeing the contents. My breath and my voice catch for a moment, but I swiftly exhale. This is right. This is what Stephen would want, for his brother to look through his things, to be comforted by them. It does so much more good than having them collect dust and sit on my bedroom floor.

I love Brendan. I love him because he has a huge heart, and I love him for his matter-of-fact approach to life. He is a pragmatic thinker at age 12, and just as his brother was, he is my teacher.

He dumps the contents of the knapsack on the bed and begins to go through them. It's all simple things really, nothing earth-shattering in the lot. And then he takes Stephen's wallet and asks me if he can go through it. I tentatively say yes, knowing that my son was, in fact, 23 years old. He pulls out student ID cards, his driver's license, and seven dollars. He pauses and says he would like to donate those seven dollars to the NC State hockey team, and I agree that it is a fantastic idea. He goes back in for more and pauses, only to stop. "What the heck?"

He pulls out a condom. The look on his face as he extracts this amazing find from the worn wallet makes me both smile and cringe with horror.

"Mom . . ."

That is all he can say at the moment. "Can I open it?"

Once again, my breath catches. But what am I to say?

"Yes," I say impulsively, not quite thinking though the implications of that decision.

He tears it open and pulls it out, examining it much like a frog in biology class. He asks questions, I trip over answers — and I mean stumble. And then it comes to me. A funny memory of "the talk" I had with Stephen about the birds and the bees. I was working in the emergency department at the time, and the poor guy received an ER nurse's graphic guide to puberty. It was one of the family jokes. He would laugh with Brady when describing it, saying he was so scared and so traumatized by my explicit and scary account of the birds and the bees, it took him years to recover.

So, as I fumbled with my hands and stumbled over every word, I could sense Stephen's amusement. I could sense that he was with us and having the greatest laugh at this extremely uncomfortable and awkward situation his mother found herself sitting in, brought to us by the condom in the wallet. I am thankful that I was honest with Brendan and focused on the memory of the "talk" rather than on the fact we were looking through my dead son's wallet.

Brendan, feeling satisfied that I had allowed him unlimited access, had enough, and off he went to play with Brady and the dog. I sat on the bed for a long time, looking at the pile of cards, the contents he kept close by, in his back pocket. I stared at his battered passport that he took everywhere. Brady and I were always pleading with him not to take it out with him to parties and such, to just use his driver's license. But he never listened. He always had it, and it showed. It looked like it had been wet previously, and the edges of the cover curled up in the shape of the letter C. I somehow think there was a story about that. He carried it everywhere. But he did not need it anymore. He was in a place where everyone knew him and his character. For that I am thankful.

Reaching down, I picked up a t-shirt from his bag. Crumpled in my hands, I brought it up to my nose and inhaled. And for a moment, he was here. With my eyes closed and smelling him, I could feel one of his hugs, the greatest hugs. Tight and intense, his hugs spoke emotion to you without words. He hugged me like that when we clung to each other after moving across Canada, he hugged me like that when our lives changed and we moved to another country, and he hugged me like that when I married Brady—and many other times in between. He would joke, say something funny or a touch sarcastic, and then hug me tight and laugh a rich laugh. And for a moment, he was here with me, embracing me and telling me it was going to be okay. It was going to get better, and one day, I may even be brave enough to move his knapsacks from my bedroom floor. One day—but not today.

Tears flowed freely as I held on to that shirt, and I simply let them. There is so much inside, and I can't hold it back. I don't want to hold it back. I want to grieve for him as he deserves.

Many one little things for this day.

July 20th: My Guardian Dear

The guardian angels of life sometimes fly so high as to be beyond our sight, but they are always looking down upon us.

~Jean Paul Richter~

Going through to the knapsack, I found an interior pocket I had not noticed before. I opened it, and inside was a wonderful gift.

A guardian angel medal I had given him rests in the palm of my hand. Cue the waterworks now. As a child, being tucked in for the night, my parents would say a prayer with me before kissing my forehead. When Stephen was born, that same prayer was taught to him—and actually, to all of the children in my family. Somewhere in my travels, I found a small medal with the prayer inscribed, and I gave it to him years ago. I always thought of that prayer in times of trouble or uncertainty in my own life. It comforted me. To this day, if I wake from a nightmare and can't get back to sleep, I say that prayer. It reminds me I am not alone, even if I am scared.

Oh Angel of God, my guardian dear.

To whom God's love commits me here.

Ever this night, be at my side.

To light and guard, to rule and guide.

Amen

Just as finding the email from him days after his death gave me comfort, finding this medal gave me solace. I was joyful, knowing that it meant something special to him and that he'd had it with him at the lake. I am thankful.

July 21st: Meditation Revelations, Hallmark Moments, and Courage

Things don't go wrong and break your heart so you can become bitter and give up. They happen to break you down and build you up so you can be all you were intended to be.

~Charlie "Tremendous" Jones~

I find that I lie in bed for about 10 minutes each morning before I get up. I'm not sure how it started; perhaps it was the initial pause I took to catch my breath or the minutes I waited to see if the pain would leave my chest. In any case, I have started to be thankful for it. It is a meditation of sorts, some time with my soul in which I gather my inner strength to go out and live another day.

It is through this meditation that I am finding myself. Sounds funny to say, as prior to July 4th, I never really thought I was lost. I felt a little unfulfilled or perhaps thought I was not living up to my true potential, but I thought I knew myself. Through the course of my life, the challenges and opportunities that I have been presented with have afforded me success and lessons, and I've always felt I was a fairly evolved person. Boy, am I learning. I have only begun my journey.

So, as I lie in bed, staring at my ceiling, I think two thoughts. First, I missed a spot when I painted the ceiling. There is a ridge there, and now that I have noticed, it will irritate me until I fix it.

Second, I am liking the Kelly I am finding in all of this hurt. I don't like how I found her, but I like her just the same. I am releasing so much: pain, hang-ups, and minutia that did nothing but overwhelm and stress me. I am shedding it because I have no room for it. In the past few weeks, I have grieved and let go of things that happened years before. I have grieved Matthew, Stephen's brother, I have let go of the pains of poor decisions, and so much more. I am letting go of the negative, whether it be thoughts, fears, mindsets, or people. I am releasing them all and wishing them luck. Because when I get caught in their story, I start to move away from my own. It is hard to explain really, but that clarity that I spoke of that came to me that morning at the lake—I know that magic, that knowing, that wisdom, that PEACE, will leave me if I let myself slip back into old habits of thinking.

And with that clarity and that wisdom, I feel Stephen. I can feel him with me, every step of the way. And when I slip back into a negative thought or speak with a negative person, he feels far away. I want him with me, even if it is only in my heart, his spirit around me. So, the shift must continue.

I have no explanation for it, only to say that I have put my faith in what God has in store for me. I knew from very early on after Stephen's passing that needed to write this, without a true understanding of why. And with each passing day, I am being given the answers.

And that, my friends, is a huge thing for a type A girl like me. Going with the flow was for rivers, garden hoses, and tap water, but not me. I made my flow. Or at least that is what I thought. What I now know is I was not making my way through the world; I was swimming against the current of my life. I was making things way too difficult, too stressful, focused on an incorrect theory of success.

I have changed. And for that I am thankful. Life has slapped me "up the side of the head," and it stings. But I feel alive.

This is something I feel tremendous gratitude for in my life today. And my acceptance of this surrendering makes me feel like I am doing right by Stephen and honoring his spirit in the best way I can. I accept what is, and I choose not to suffer because of it. I choose to learn from it.

Brendan and I spent a little time in Stephen's room today. We go in for short spurts and then quickly leave, feeling as if we may suffocate and that the air has been taken out of the room. It is funny, as one of us will say, "Okay, that's enough." And we simply leave. It feels good to be strong enough to go in there, but it is difficult. We are taking little steps.

So, on our visit today, we found a couple of treasures. I could smile through the tears, as I read one particular note, telling him how special he was, how we believed in him and knew he could do anything. I thought back to the moment I wrote those words: the day he was leaving for college. I wanted him to know that I was so proud of him, and I was humbled by how wonderful he was, as I felt I had been such an imperfect parent. I gave the card to him as he was getting into his car to leave for school. I was standing in the garage, and I slipped it into his hand as we hugged tightly and said goodbye. I was trying to be strong and told him I loved him and was so proud of him. I told him he was going to do so well at school and that this was his time. He kissed my cheek, told me he loved me, and turned to walk towards the car.

And as he turned to begin the next chapter of his own life, a chapter of my own was concluding. And I was not ready for it. I wanted to protest it and have him come back in the house and unpack his bags. He needed to stay, as I could keep him safe here. I wanted to tell him that because of my youth that we had not had enough time together, as I had been busy with school or had been immature or not old enough to understand the swift passage of time that adults seem to know all too well. But I could not say that nor make that request. It was time, and I could see how eager he was to begin this journey. He jumped in the car, and I tried to give a supportive wave, but the tears started, and the face contorted. I am terrible at crying. I don't look like the people in the movies who can cry and still look ravishing. I snort and sob, and it is not at all glamorous.

And sitting in the driver's seat, he looked up and saw me. And he put the car in park and jumped out and came towards me with his arms extended. He hugged me deeply and whispered in my ear, "I love you, Mom. We will see each other soon. I love you very much, and I am not far away."

Looking down at the card and reliving that memory, I am touched deeply by the words. For just as he said those words in reference to his move to Raleigh and beginning university, he could say the same words to me if he could speak to me right now.

I love you, Mom. We will see each other soon. I love you very much, and I am not far away.

I am thankful. And I do believe he is not far away. He is with me.

Brendan finds some game footage, and we take a moment to watch Stephen playing university hockey. I am thankful we have this record, and we can see him, playing, with a gracefulness in the net that did not seem to match the sport.

So, thank you. I have gratitude for insight, for memories, good and loving memories, and for courage and resilience. I am learning.

July 22nd: The Weight of Sadness and the Letter

Beauty that dies the soonest has the longest life. Because it cannot keep itself for a day, we keep it forever. Because it can have existence only in memory, we give it immortality there.

~Bertha Louise (Clark) Damon~

I know that every single day is not going to be a good one. I am realistic. I understand it, and as I have said before, I am accepting of the ache. I cannot change it, and I will not fight it. But that does not mean I have to enjoy it. Today is a painful day.

All day, I've felt like I could not move. I am tired—exhausted actually—and I just can't get out of my own way. I look at things around the house, and I cry. Brendan is sleeping late, and I am thankful for that, as I don't want him to see me completely falling apart. I am feeling that I was incorrect in my assessment of my personal resilience. I don't think I can actually move on from this. I was delusional in thinking I could because I had survived all the other struggles in my life, bounced back from things in the past stronger and wiser. Not this time. Today, I feel like the best course of action would be to lie down and just give up.

I feel shameful for saying that, and I don't know why. I am allowed to feel that way; it should be no surprise that a day like this would come. But for some reason, I feel that wallowing is not part of the path. This is not how I get through this; this is how I get stuck. I am not saying that these moments are not part of grief, but I am saying that I cannot let myself be in this emotional place for a prolonged period of time. This dark space can only breed anger and bitterness for me, and I promised myself that would not happen. But I can't help myself.

I lie quietly on the couch, staring off at the wall, quiet for well over an hour. The story of my misfortune replays in my mind over and over. There is nothing good that can come from this, only bad. Maybe what I've been reading is true. Maybe I should be asking the same question that others ask on those grief message boards. Maybe I should be asking why God wanted to punish me. Why did He let this happen?

But that does not seem right. That question does not fit. Because I don't think God did let this happen. I think it just happened.

Thankfully, Brendan wakes from his slumber and drags me away from my dark thoughts. So, on this dark day, I am thankful for Brendan. He is a gift. He has an ability, without words, to realign me with the real view of the world, and with the goodness that exists within it. He serves as an important reminder for me, so I will say thank you for him today.

But despite his smile and the sparkle in his eyes, I cannot shake the shawl of sadness from my shoulders.

It is a quiet day, and I busy myself with the mundane but find myself sluggish. And with each passing hour, I am more frustrated with my outlook and wish I had more power over my emotions. I feel like I am falling down a deep hole and I can't stop it, nor did I bring a shovel to dig out.

I walk outside to get the mail, and the warmth of the Carolina sun hits my face. I usually celebrate this fantastic gift, but today, it is too hot, too humid, too far away from my family. I look quickly up and down the street, not wanting to see anyone or talk to any of my neighbors. Thankfully, it is quiet, and human interaction will not interrupt the pity party I am throwing for myself.

And then it shifts. In the mail, a plain envelope, addressed to Brady and me. And inside is a gift from Ben, one of Stephen's friends. This gift will not only shift my perspective for the day but is something I will carry with me for months and years to come.

This boy took the time to type a five-page letter to Brady, Brendan, and me. The content was personal and funny and heartbreaking all at the same time. It told me stories of his relationship with Stephen that I had not known and added strokes to the pictures of my boy I had painted in my mind. Just as the words of those brave enough to speak at the memorial helped me see the Stephen they saw, this letter told me a beautiful story. It was a story of Stephen, fun and goofy, living life to the fullest, enjoying every minute of the university experience and touching the lives of people like Ben. It was honest, and I found myself at times laughing out loud while crying at the same time. It did not paint a picture of him as a saint, because he wasn't. It was real. It was not an obituary or a speech or a greeting card, where someone is glorified. It was a simple picture of a friendship and what it meant.

I will write to him to thank him, but I am not sure if he will ever truly understand what his letter did for me. He will never understand how his words gave us strength, how his words to Brendan helped him understand that he still had a connection with the team and with his friends. He will never understand how his words to Brady about his relationship with Stephen not only provided comfort but provided Brady with a validation that others saw how remarkable and special their bond was, having only known each other for a short period of time.

With his permission, here it is:

Dear Kelly and Brady,

I would like to say I'm very sorry, as losing Stephen is a big loss to everyone. The reason I am writing this is because of my lack of speaking at Stephen's memorial service. I did not speak because I knew I would get through saying "Stephen" and then start bawling and I wouldn't be able to get out what I really wanted to say. I know this cause even walking into the house was tough. Everywhere I looked I saw Stephen. Whether it was where he always parked his car to the Christmas tree that stayed up till like March to the "artwork" we got at Goodwill, or late nights in the kitchen. Everywhere I turned in that house I would think of a good time I had with Stephen. So, I wanted to share with you guys those good stories that I have about Stephen and the joy he brought. I also want to share what Stephen meant to me and everyone around him. I would like to tell you that this could get pretty long because there are so many stories, so take a seat in a nice and comfy chair. I also want to let you know that I am an engineering student, so I have bad grammar and jump around a lot so bear with me.

I guess I will start from the beginning of knowing Stephen, which was obviously his first year on the team. That first year was a year of learning about him and all the goalie quirks he had. He was quiet the first year and I thought he was just one of those quiet and goofy goalies that just want to be by themselves. Let's just say I was way off on that.

I remember the road trips that year when Phil and I would usually follow Stephen and Ross in a car to wherever we were going. I could never really understand how two goalies battling for playing time could be friends, but who knows. Anyway, on the road trips, I had to do all the driving in my car, and Stephen doing the most with him and Ross since we both had stick and no one else could ever figure out how to drive stick. We would try to lose each other and do stuff like faking an exit and what not. The thing I remember most though is this. It was about 2 or 3 in the morning after the game. We were driving home, and I noticed Stephen started to weave from side to side, but he kept on going. Finally, we stopped at a rest stop, and I asked him about it. He said, "Yeah, I'm a little tired, but I figured it would help you stay awake, worrying about me." That first year, I also remember how serious he was and how important hockey was to him. You could not say the wrong thing to him on game day because game day was his day. By the way, who got him the roller bag? Let's just say he got a little heat for that in the locker room.

The next year we started to hang out a lot more. I think it really started after one morning practice. Stephen was one of the last ones out of the dressing room, like usual, and I was hanging around. We started talking hockey and what not and came up with a brilliant idea to take our conversation to IHOP. We got there and heard they had a $4.99 breakfast, so we were game. But, for some reason, we felt that something that cost only $4.99 would not be filling enough because we just came from practice. So, we got two each. On top of that, Stephen orders the biggest Apple Juice they had, which was a carafe of juice. We got all of our food, and then realized what a mistake we had made because on the hockey team, we have a rule that you have to finish what you order. We set out to finish our meals. Three hours, two bathroom breaks and one waitress later we both finished our meals. That whole time I think we talked about hockey. We also decided that going to class that day was not going to be an option, as we were going to spend the rest of the day on the toilet.

Going to IHOP after Thursday morning practice quickly became a tradition for us. We always had our same waitress, Teresa. She would have our drinks waiting for us and was always excited to see us. We even carried that tradition over to Florida Gulf Coast University because after Stephen stood on his head we decided to go to Denny's. While there, a guy came up to us and said some girls wanted to give this napkin to us. It had their number on it and they recognized Stephen and they wanted to talk to us. We were completely speechless and needless to say that made our night. We did in fact have to call them the next day. Our bus broke down, so we were able to convince them to drive thirty minutes out of their way to come pick us up and drop us off at our hotel. We never talked to them again, but they did love Stephen's Canadian charm. Stephen also got a Facebook friend request a month later from some girl at FGCU, and she would send him messages and write on his wall. Stephen left quite an impression, not only on the coaches and players that game, but also on the females watching as well.

That game was one of the best games I had ever seen Stephen play. It took him at least a half an hour to get undressed because he was so tired. Two other games that come to mind that season were when we played Kennesaw State and Liberty. In those games, Stephen knew what he had to do, and that was basically stand on his head if we were to have a chance to win. He took that challenge and stared it right down and played better than any other goalie in the league. While in one of those games, I may not have been very helpful, but I was always extremely proud to go talk to someone and say, "Yeah, that's my team's goalie and he is one of my best friends."

Another thing Stephen and I did that year was to go to the State Fair, just the two of us, which may seem pretty lame, but it was by far the best time I have ever had at a fair. We played all the games and spent close to $50.00 a piece on silly carnival games like break the glass bottle. But we each came out with a playboy bunny pillow. Those were probably the most expensive playboy bunny pillows out there, but they are also the most memorable. Stephen was able to come out with a little something extra though, an admirer. Her name was Dawn, and she was in her late 40's. Somehow, she started talking to us, and we talked to her about hockey and what not. One thing led to another, and she grabbed Stephen's butt. I'm not sure Stephen was ever the same after that experience. Apparently, grabbing Stephen wasn't enough, because she came to one of our games. After the game, we were terrified that she would be waiting for us, so we made sure we went out in a group.

We also played racquetball all the time. Stephen started out slow, as he did not receive his training from the great NC State Racquetball classes yet, but he still put forth his best and would run after balls that seemed unachievable. I have never seen someone dive onto a hard wooden floor as much as I saw Stephen do it. It just showed how much he cared about what he was doing and how much he wanted to win. By the end of the year, he was starting to beat me, and I did not know what to do. The only thing I could think of was to hit him "accidentally" with the ball. It would sting him a little, but he would still pull out a victory and also respond with his own "accidental" hit. So, we would end up with bruises and marks all over and they were not from playing hockey. Those games got so intense that one day I was able to win and celebrate my victory. I decided to drive all the way to Toys 'R' Us to get a wrestling belt that said I was the champion. Stephen was in the car with me and had no clue where I was going but was cool with it. Once we found the belts, Stephen decided that if I was going to be the World Champion, he was going to be the Intercontinental Champion. Then we decided that while we were at it, we should get tag team belts, as we made a pretty good team too. At the end of it, we had four kids' belts and more fun than any kid could ever have.

Another great memory of Stephen is the Christmas party. As you guys are well aware, we had some pretty sweet outfits including pipes (thanks Brady). You guys probably also knew that Stephen was my Secret Santa. He got me some funny things and some things digging into my past, but it was Stephen so I couldn't be mad for long. We had a lot of fun that night. Stephen and I made it home but lost Phil. I told Stephen to sleep in Phil's room. The next morning, I walk into Phil's room and Stephen is sleeping in his closet. I asked him why and he said he didn't want to sleep in Phil's bed and the closet looked comfortable. Another moment I will never forget as Stephen did things that you could not explain but put a smile on your face.

Here are some random facts about Stephen:

Favorite Song: Mortal Kombat Theme Song

Helped create a drink called the CanUSA

Late night Taco Bell was a favorite

Known to Sing in the Shower

A very skilled Mario Kart 64 Player

Great at thinking of Secret Santa Gifts

Ate any food given to him, no matter how burnt it was.

Could jump really, really high.

Hockey has been interlaced through a lot of these stories, so I think it's time to talk about it. We all know how much it meant to Stephen. When the team found out about this goalie from Canada, we thought he better be good, and he lived up to it. I think we would have lowered those expectations if we knew he only started playing hockey at the age of 12. Most of us have been playing hockey since we were 5. For him to start so late and still be as good as he was; it was amazing. We would tell the coaches and players on any team we played that he started that late, and they would laugh at us and say you can't do that. But Stephen did do it and was cool to see him do it.

One of the reasons that Stephen was able to be so successful was the fact that he was so intense and cared about what he did. He always wanted to stop the puck, no matter if it was the 200th shot he faced at practice, or a one goal with one minute left in the third. He was going to stop that puck. The preparation that Stephen went through was also amazing and quite entertaining. On game days, everything had to go to plan. He had to eat the right things, watch the right videos, drink his red Gatorade, and make sure his clothes were ironed. All of it had to be just so before we left for the rink. Once we got to the rink, it was Stephen's time, no matter if he was starting or not. And nobody minded because they knew the results that his rituals produced.

Stephen also made other people better because even though he was a goalie, he would get on you if you were not working hard or taking bad penalties. I got my fair share of scolding from Stephen. I didn't mind them because I knew Stephen cared and that he had one of the best hockey minds on the team even though he never played out. As you know, Stephen was not very happy with the number of penalties that I took and he probably got pissed at me more than anyone, and it was deserved. But, for some reason, I could never change my bad ways. This season it is my goal to lessen my penalty minutes dramatically because I know how much Stephen hated it, and every time I go in the box he will be looking down and shaking his finger at me. I want to say I will try my best, but I will not promise his finger won't be shaking at me a few times. My game will not only be different in less penalty minutes, but it will also be a step up. Because I know Stephen will be right there along side of me telling me exactly what to do or not do, as he will be with every other player on the team. So, when you see NC State Hockey have one of its best seasons, know that even though your son is not on the roster, he is the reason we are winning.

Our hockey talk was not just limited to NC State Hockey. The Bruins and Canadiens was usually a daily topic. Depending on whose team was doing better, that person would always bring it up. If both teams were sucking, our conversation wouldn't last too long. But, as much as I hate to say it, I intend to carry on some of Stephen's passion for the Canadiens, as long as they aren't playing the Bruins.

There are so many more good stories with Stephen, it's hard not to think of all the good times we had. Stephen became like a brother to me. I was able to talk to him about anything, joke about anything, and I was always having fun when I was around him. Stephen would not let things get him down even if they didn't go his way. He wouldn't let anyone else around him get down either. If the situation looked bad, Stephen would find a way to turn it around, and make sure everyone was happy. As crazy as it sounds about quiet Stephen, he was the life of the party and made sure he enjoyed his life every moment.

Stephen was fiercely competitive no matter what we were playing. Whether it was Jeopardy, Bocce Ball, NHL '96, Racquetball, or hockey, Stephen always wanted to win. But what made him really unique was despite his competitiveness, if he lost, he would be just as happy as if he won and would celebrate with you . . .. which would kind of take the thrill out of winning. But it made it really good to be around him.

It was a real pleasure to spend a few years with Stephen and he is a person I will never forget and will always keep in my heart. Stephen was one of the best people I have ever met, and you should be proud of how he was raised. Kelly, he loved you so much and he knew you were always there for him and how much you loved him. The relationship you guys had is something every mother and son wants to achieve. Brady, Phil, and I were talking, and we had to stop and think that you were not always with Stephen, in his life. The relationship you two had was amazing, it was like you had always been part of his life and the two of you were best friends since he was born. Please also let Brendan know that he was so important to Stephen and how much Stephen loved him... Tell him that he is always welcome to skate with the NC State Hockey team anytime he wants. Stephen touched everyone he met, and he will be missed dearly, but know what a great affect he had on everybody and what a great affect you guys had on him.

Love,

Ben Dombrowski

Just as things always seem to happen, it came to me at the very moment I needed it most, as if someone was watching out for us and had a bag full of comfort to hand out at just the right moment, when we could not see the goodness and needed some help. I think someone may be watching out for us. Just maybe.

I am thankful. Because the magic and mystery of life, even when I lose faith in it from time to time, is still there.

July 24th: Butterflies and Belief

Life is eternal; and love is immortal; and death is only a horizon; and a horizon is nothing save the limit of our sight.

~Rossiter Worthington Raymond~

So many butterflies have surrounded me in the past few weeks. It is hard for me to explain it. I've read that butterflies have been identified for thousands of years as a creature that plays a role in bridging the gap between life and death. Many of the ancient civilizations believed that butterflies were symbols of the human soul. There are variations in the interpretation, from the Irish to the Maya, but the theme is similar and the relationship between life and death undeniable. The Aztecs, in particular, believed that the happy dead in the form of beautiful butterflies would visit their relatives to assure them that all was well and that they were happy on the other side.

I have no evidence-based rationale for what is happening around me, but I believe it. I guess it is kind of like faith; I've learned a lot about my beliefs lately—what I, through my own independent choice, decide to accept as true. Faith is choosing to trust in something even if you can't see it or explain it, even if others tell you something different or express doubt. So, I will have faith. Just as I know that gratitude is what will save me from this dark time, I also know that all those butterflies are no coincidence.

Today I am thankful for butterflies, making me feel that I am surrounded by a love that is unseen but ever present.

July 25th: The Wisdom from the Bags on the Floor

Gratitude bestows reverence, allowing us to encounter everyday epiphanies, those transcendent moments of awe that change forever how we experience life and the world.

~John Milton~

The quiet of a Saturday morning, where the only agenda you need to worry about is your own. Free Saturdays don't come often in our house, especially during hockey season, but in the warm days of summer, they are all mine.

Waking before anyone else, I once again spend some time with my thoughts and looking at the bags on the floor. Yes, I know I need to unpack them. I need to move them from my bedroom. I need to put them away but not yet. I am not ready, and I am okay with that. The bags—where his hands touched, where he left one of his last marks on the world. I somehow feel his presence is evaporating like the morning mist. Did he know, did he feel anything as he packed his things? Those two bags have been the first things I have looked at in the morning and the last things at night. They are tangible proof that he existed. The bags are confirmation—a piece of him and his touch on the world.

I am not ready to undo that.

I've looked through the contents, and I've thought a lot about his thoughts as he packed the bag in anticipation. As I did with my father's death, I wonder if he had a feeling, an unconscious knowing, that this was it, that it was his time. Did he feel the angels circling? I have no answers.

In that email exchange I have written so much about, I keep remembering the line where he said, **"I want more than anything to have some epiphany one day where everything is laid out for me and there is no more second-guessing or decisions to be made for my career path, but I can't force it I guess."**

I've thought a lot about those words, about how they relate to life. Is it that he could not see things laid out before him because God had a much bigger plan? I will never have an answer, but I wonder like that these days. I wonder if he did not press the questions because on some level, he was aware the answers were not necessary or had been taken care of.

As a consequence of my ponderings since Stephen's death, I am looking at my own life questions that I have not yet answered. We all sit here in this life and plan to do things—to be happy, to achieve all those goals and dreams on our list, to right wrongs or call that family member we've been avoiding. With the exception of those who lay on their death beds, ravaged by disease, their expiration date confirmed by medical specialists, aren't we all walking through this life of ours like we have infinite time? Time to be happy, to lose the weight, write the book, make a mark on the world, to feel good about yourself, forgive those who've hurt you. For most of us, we look away from the things that truly are most meaningful and instead obsess about the worthless and the details that will be of no consequence when we are faced with the end of our life here on earth. I have to take responsibility for doing all of the above in one way or another at points in my life. Those bags, sitting on a now dusty floor, teach me lessons every morning I look at them. Every day, having them in my field of vision sparks a different thought, a new point to reflect upon. They are my inanimate teachers, and I am showing up every morning for the lesson.

I am thankful for those lessons.

I have some emotional work to do. But I am going to heal and live. And when I am finally at the end of my time here on earth and when I see Stephen again, I want to tell him, "You were my epiphany."

Thank you for the insights given to me by a Roots knapsack. Thank you for the epiphany of Stephen. Thank you for allowing me to finally be ready to learn.

July 27th: Dream, Dream, Dream

Gratitude unlocks the fullness of life. It turns what we have into enough, and more. It turns denial into acceptance, chaos to order, confusion to clarity. It can turn a meal into a feast, a house into a home, a stranger into a friend. Gratitude makes sense of our past, brings peace for today, and creates a vision for tomorrow.

~Melody Beattie~

I love my dreams. In them, he can still be here with me, and I have had the greatest visions now two nights in a row. In them, he is talking to me. They are weird and disconnected, as dreams go. In one, I am planning his funeral but yet, at one point, we sneak away to talk about something, just the two of us. Last night, here were the words I took, "Mom, what I've learned is that many people go through life and miss 9–1, completely." The dreams come to me, perhaps from my exhaustive REM sleep. The past few weeks are catching up to me, and I am really fatigued, both from the travel and the simple act of grieving. I have opened myself to it, and it takes all that I have. But the weariness is welcomed because I am facing the truth and learning from it.

In the dream, missing a great part of the day resonates with me. I have spent many portions of my life distracting myself from what hurt me. I've missed so much time running from the truth, the pain. But now, I feel softened and vulnerable and open, and I am allowing the truth in, and it hurts terribly. I am awake for each moment of the day, and I am giving thanks for all that I am learning.

I think it is Stephen guiding me to this place, continuing to be my teacher.

So, today I am thankful for my words, my wakefulness, and the clarity I have received from my hurt. I am thankful for dreams that allow me to have one more conversation.

July 28th: Taking Care of Each Other

There is a sacredness in tears. They are not the mark of weakness, but of power. They speak more eloquently than ten thousand tongues. They are the messengers of overwhelming grief . . . and of unspeakable love.

~Washington Irving~

3,000 pairs of socks. Stephen had so many pairs of socks, and I'm not sure how that happened. As Brendan and I rummage through a few more boxes, we discover more treasures from his life. At moments, it is consoling, and at others, it is not. Rather than comfort, I feel like an unknown force is clenching my heart beneath his strong fingers, squeezing the life out of it, the joy dripping from the ends of his fingertips.

I cannot help myself, and I smell one of his shirts. And when the olfactory senses kick in and spark memories from his scent, my face contorts, squeezes up like I am a raisin, and the tears flow freely. The good news is Brendan seems to have made peace with my crying periodically. We've discussed that it is okay to cry. He tells me he loves me, or hugs me, I compose myself, and we continue on with our day. I am thankful for that. I am pleased that I can weep in front of him, and he understands it is a normal response to losing Stephen. We talked about it, and he is not alarmed. He does not leave the room to get away from it. He stays—close. I am glad that we are working through this together, instead of alone, behind closed doors, hiding our pain. I believe it helps him as well, and he knows what he is feeling inside is a normal response.

We talk quietly as we find things. Some make us laugh, others make us quiet, and we quickly move on to the next object. It is an unspoken understanding between my boy and me about how to handle this. We are the keepers of the other's heart, and we step tentatively while in this room, to protect the other. Today we stayed here for about an hour. Other days it has been mere minutes. And some days, we don't even have the courage to open the door. But it is all good.

I am thankful for those moments with my boy. I want Brendan to drink up the parts of Stephen's personality and spirit that sit in these boxes. I want him to hold on to them and have his brother in his heart as he grows. Perhaps, in some way, it will comfort him when he can't have that conversation after a hockey game or that big brother support when he faces those tough teenage dating scenarios.

I am thankful for this exercise in grief, as it is allowing us to revisit moments from our past and relive the good and the bad with a new perspective. I am grateful, for the truth is, I have mostly good memories. I am thankful for each item in these boxes, as they give us an opportunity to take a journey back to those moments and be appreciative for the life we did have with a wonderful boy.

July 29th: Falling to Pieces and Being Put Back Together by Faith

Perhaps love is like a resting place, a shelter from the storm. It exists to give you comfort. It is there to keep you warm. And in those times of trouble, when you are most alone, the memory of love will bring you home.

~John Denver~

It may sound weird, but my one little thing today was having a couple hours to myself where I simply fell apart. I cried as I had at the water's edge, from the depths of my soul, chanting Stephen's name. I just needed to let some of the "ache" out of me. Because boy, do I ache. I am focused on the present and finding peace and purpose. But that doesn't mean I don't feel the pain. In fact, I believe because I am facing it head on, in some ways I am "feeling it" even more because I'm not looking away from it. I've made the decision to see it for what it really is, to walk through the valley and not around it as such, but it is a pain like I've never felt before.

My heart throbs. I keep talking about the good things to embrace in my life, because I am trying to convince myself that they are not just figments of my imagination. I am trying to convince myself that good can still exist in the middle of such pain. Through my tears, I feel that if I can prove this to be true, I will be honoring the life of Stephen. I am human and have wondered at times how I will go on, wanting to see him again desperately. If God would only be merciful and let me have one more moment. Stephen was my child, but he was also with me for more than half my life. Imagine that: I was a child, and so was he. I've had more of my life with him than without, and of all the people in my life, he and I had the most history. And now, I have to figure out what my life means without him in it physically.

I believe my tears will tell me. With each drop that flows endlessly from my eyes, rolling down my cheeks, I am figuring it out. For that, I am thankful.

As I had some alone time, I quietly went to Stephen's room, wanting to look through his belongings privately. Being alone with his things aided the flow of tears. I found papers from school, projects from the fifth grade, silly things that sparked memories and more waterworks. I don't know what I am looking for, some sort of message, some "moment" or communication that will confirm that part of him is still with me. Perhaps some note that outlines everything that he felt and thought about. You know — nothing too elaborate, just the secrets of the universe.

And as with every other moment in the day, I am thinking about what I believe in, what I have faith in, and what I know for sure.

I feel hardly qualified to write about faith. Not because I'm not a faithful person; I am, now more than any other time in my life. I think it may be related to my on and off again connection with my faith leading up to this life change. I certainly don't feel like an expert. But the more I think about it, the more I realize I really am qualified. Sure, I would lose terribly if I was in a theological discussion with some of the respected religious leaders of this world. But I now believe I understand faith, at least in a personal sense.

The reason? Because at the darkest moment, I held on. I felt I had lost everything; my beautiful son was gone. But even though I had questions for God, I still held on to my faith in Him. With everything stripped away, it was truly the only thing that remained. Nothing else could give me comfort or peace. My faith was the only thing I still believed in. I say that, knowing I had a loving and stupendous husband holding me up, a beautiful younger son who loves large, and family and friends like no other. But truly, at the moment I realized Stephen was dead, and for many moments after that day, my faith is what has permitted me to accept the truth with a peace in my heart.

It was as if God said, "I know it is pretty bad. I know a lot of people will find it too painful to be around you because they don't know what to say, and it hurts. But I love you and I am not going anywhere." In my heart and mind, I did not feel that anyone really knew how I felt—only God.

And since then, we talk daily. I know my relationship with God does not fit into one of the neat and very confined denominational boxes. But somehow, I know that is a good thing. I am afraid, as I have never been connected in this way before, but I trust that we will work it out. A bumper sticker I saw once sums it up nicely:

"God doesn't call the qualified, He qualifies the called."

Today, I am thankful for being connected to a wisdom that once eluded me. I am thankful for the faith I have and the knowing that Stephen is okay and that we will be okay too. I am thankful that I believe this is part of a bigger story that I do not yet understand. I am most grateful that I am choosing to continue to live and watch how this story unfolds.

July 30th: The Grief Lady and Taking the Leap

Friends are angels who lift us to our feet when our wings have trouble remembering how to fly.

~Author Unknown~

I've never been one to ask for help with things, but today I had my first appointment with our counselor, Clarisse. I have walked my path alone for many of the hardships in my life, and most times, it was to my own detriment. People need to be able to ask for help and to lean on others; that has been a hard lesson for me to learn, but I am glad I finally understand. Because I have no idea how to cope with this, I need help.

As I drove to the appointment, I laughed to myself, wondering if this poor woman knew what she was in for with me. The plan was to have me meet with her first, and then Brendan would see her in the afternoon. My initial thought was that I would meet with her and fill her in on how the family was coping, how we were doing, what things I was hoping to achieve from the sessions. I even took the time to draw out a chart, explaining all of the family dynamics and our vision and goals for the sessions. Yes, I did that.

I arrived at her office, anxious to get started. I felt immediately at ease after meeting her. I sat in the comfy chair and immediately took a pillow to hold on to for comfort. And she asked me one simple question, and my well-thought-out agenda went out the window. Any hope of intelligent conversation based on my family dynamics chart or goals fell by the wayside as I cried, sobbed, snorted, and blubbered. I told her the story of Stephen, from beginning to end. And it was healing. To just let it all out. To just let it flow out without me feeling I had to control the message, or keep strong, or follow an agenda. It was nothing like I had planned, but it was exactly what I needed. And the most beautiful thing? She, at points, cried with me. It was the most empathetic and beautiful thing I have ever experienced from someone. She was professional and kind all at the same time, and there are so many who could take a lesson from her.

I am thankful.

Later that afternoon, Brendan had his first appointment. It was a big step for both of us, and we felt good after it was over. Without prompting, he said, "I like her" as we walked across the parking lot. And it was at that moment that he first used the title that would make me smile for weeks to come:

"The Grief Lady."

I love 12-year-old minds. I am not sure how she would feel about it, but I have a hunch she would be fine with us injecting some levity into our difficult days.

July 31st: Bathtub Reflections and Time

Nothing valuable can be lost by taking time.

~Abraham Lincoln~

I woke early and read for a while in the bathtub. I've always loved that quiet, early morning, when it is just me and my thoughts. I have contemplated many things in my life from the comfort of my bath. There is a great window that allows me to look out at the backyard. It is private and inviting, and the yard has a little of Stephen at every corner. Our *inukshuk*, built from leftover stone used in our landscaping, designed as a marker for our family. The Inuit used it as a tool for navigation, a point of reference to communicate that it was a safe place to camp or a good hunting ground. We built it to remind ourselves that this was our haven, our safe spot to return to where you would always be welcomed, nurtured, and loved.

As I gaze out the window, I think about God coming for breakfast. If only He could show up, no invitation required. I would have strawberries and blueberries, with low-fat vanilla yogurt and Kashi cereal sprinkled on the top. I'm sure He/She would like it. And green tea. For some reason, I think God drinks green tea. I'm reading *The Shack* and wishing that I could have a meeting like that one. But it is a book. And although I love the message within it, I understand I have to find peace in my own shack or at my own cove at Jordan Lake.

I will find peace. And I will find purpose. I believe there is something in all of this—the writing, the trying to stay positive even in the bleakest of circumstances. I think this is part of the purpose, but it is too soon to tell. So, I will continue to go with the flow of things, as I have been since the 4th of July. Because I don't know if it is Stephen or God or both, but I feel like I am not driving the bus. And that works for me right now.

But bigger than that, it is the knowledge that time spent with your child, however frivolous it may seem when your list is long, is worth more than anything else in the world. All of our crazy projects, watching that movie, our late-night chats—they are more precious to me now than any accolades received professionally, more than any time I have given away to life's worries or annoyances. I am thankful.

August 1st: Sun-Drenched Lazy Days of Summer

Happiness is as a butterfly which, when pursued, is always beyond our grasp, but which, if you will sit down quietly, may alight upon you.

~Nathaniel Hawthorne~

I love being in the water. It is so peaceful. I read a few things about families that stay away from the water after losing someone to a drowning. I just can't do that—not to Brendan, or me. Helen Keller said, "Security is mostly a superstition. It does not exist in nature, nor do the children of men as a whole experience it. Avoiding danger is no safer in the long run than outright exposure. Life is either a daring adventure or nothing."

Now, if you want to look at someone who made a conscious decision to be happy in spite of adversity and challenge in her life, Helen Keller would be your girl. And I agree with her. There is a plan bigger than all of us; I have come to know that now. So, whether we are in or out of the water, it makes no difference. That statement is not defeatist. In fact, I say that with the most resilience I can muster at this point. We choose to live, and live we will, even if we have to force ourselves to do so for a little while. We choose to climb trees, just as Stephen did, scrape knees, and ride our bikes into the waves. And when I finally get called home and see my child again, I want to be able to tell God, "I used it all, everything you gave me". And I want HIM to tell me I did good.

Today I am thankful for resilience and courage and knowing that Brendan deserves to have a happy life that is not in a bubble. I can do this.

August 2nd: Insight, Forgiveness, Harry Potter, and God's Plan

To bring up a child in the way he should go, travel that way yourself once in a while.

~Josh Billings~

The day before my birthday. 29 again this year. Ah, no, not this year. I feel that I could be turning 100. I feel like an old woman this year. But I am still here. I still am surrounded by love, and I still have the most loving little boy.

I've got to work to find one little thing. I only cried a couple of times today, and both were when I was writing about something particularly painful. I still physically ache, and I am not being a Pollyanna, but I feel that my focus on these "one little things" has helped shine a light for me in the darkness. It has kept me focused on the fact that there is still a lot of good in the world—a lot of beauty and a lot of life left to live. Amazing. I sound like Stuart Smalley from *Saturday Night Live*. I'm good enough, I'm strong enough, and doggone it, people like me.

I am still reading *The Shack*. It is changing my perspective, and it is assisting me with this internal conversation I am having with The Big Guy. I say that having read some of the reviews about the book and its departure from religious doctrine. I wish everyone would take a deep breath. The world moves so fast these days. I find that as fast as someone puts a thought out there, someone is chasing them down to discredit it. If only the scholars of the world could only share their knowledge with ink and quill, maybe it would give some more time for people to absorb the words prior to judging. I find it all very tiring. I have actually stopped watching the news and reading the newspaper. At least for a little while.

Prior to Stephen's death, I was not so much having a crisis in faith. I was actually reading the Bible and exploring my faith more than I ever had before. But I always had this sort of inferiority complex about the whole thing. That has changed. Looking at it from my shifted perspective, I can now see clearly that my insecurity in faith had nothing to do with God. Rather, it was with the interpretations of the various religions of what God means to the world. It did not make sense, to see someone present themselves as righteous and pious, but their outward behavior and treatment did not appear to be Christian. I am including myself in this analogy. It is truly about walking the talk, and I struggled in finding peace with the version of God I was being presented with. But I think I have it figured out now, if only for myself. For me, I no longer feel the need to look outward towards the various religions and organized churches to tell me what God is for me. It is personal. And because it is so personal and between the two us, I could go to any church in the world and now feel like I belonged.

My daily reflections keep going back to faith. But truly, how else could I find gratitude in grief without faith? I dig out an email I received from Stephen in April. He was exploring his faith in the spring, and he and I had some wonderful conversations. Here's what he said:

During Jesus' lifetime, he did not look up to those wealthier than him, or those who spent all of their days worshiping in temples, he cared about the type of person you were. He ate with tax collectors, the most hated people of his time, and it did not matter to him. On his last days of living, a prostitute was by his side as he was approaching death and his eventual resurrection. If we are called to be good Christians, which is to essentially be more like Jesus (we can never achieve his status, all we can do is strive to be better Christians in his eyes), how do we do it? Going to church every Sunday does not make you a good Christian automatically, it is how you live your life, and whether or not you accept faith and Jesus into your heart . . . . . That is what makes you a true believer . . . . . Stephen P. Russell - April 2009-

I will admit: Reading this makes me sad a little, and I do wonder why someone like this had to go so soon. I am humbled by his perspective and will carry it forward with me.

Anyway, as I continue to read *The Shack*, I pause, and I meditate on a certain thought or concept and try to figure out a reasonable application with what I am dealing with. Today I was thinking about a person who played a big part in Stephen's and my life but who treated him wrong. And there was a lot left unsaid. I am struggling with it, as I have been wondering if I should be the one to make sure the message is conveyed. The whole thing ties me in a knot, to be honest. So, today, I just had a conversation with God and Stephen about it all. And I feel like I am figuring out the answer. That is a "one little thing".

Finally, Brendan and I went to see *Harry Potter and the Half-Blood Prince*. Great movie, even if I did not really understand some parts. But it was a joy to just be with Brendan, and it was the first real place I had ventured to outside of the house, other than to church. Up to this point, I have spent a lot of time at home. In the dark of the theater, Brendan and I held hands, and I could sense that it made him feel good.

On the drive home, we were talking about Stephen, and the topic of God's plan came up. And Brendan said that he was wondering about God's plan and what the purpose would be in this happening. And I was honest. I did not know. I told him I did not know if Stephen dying was part of God's plan, but I did believe that part of His purpose and His plan is to make sure that He takes care of us as we miss Stephen and surrounds us with lots of love. And I do believe that God must have needed him for something really special. But all of that felt quite insufficient, and I simply don't feel I have the qualifications to speak on behalf of God.

So, I explained it in the best way I could and then offered him an example. "Brendan, do you remember how I told you how I had Stephen when I was younger?" I asked.

"Yes," he said.

"Well, Brendan, as you can imagine, I was a teenager, with all my friends and music and school, and when I found out I was pregnant, I thought my life was absolutely over. I believed that everything had ended, and there would be no joy left in anything I did. It was the worst thing! As far as God's will and plan, I could not understand."

He nodded, listening attentively.

"But when Stephen came, I could see it. I could feel that he was meant to be here and was part of something special, something much bigger than me or school dances or music lessons. Today, as your mom looks at things, I can see that when Stephen arrived, just like you, they were the two best things that ever happened to me. And 23 years later, I can see just how intricate and special God's plan really was. Think about all the people who have emailed us, called us, sent us cards, posted on Facebook. All of those people have been touched and affected by Stephen. Think about all the people he helped or loved or was kind to; think about what he did for all of us. That is what I believe God's plan was. I think God knew how Stephen would touch so many people, and how much joy his life would bring to the world."

I exhaled. I had a proud and momentous smile. I was a damn good parent. My God, we had just had a moment. I was feeling pretty good about myself and was, for once, not feeling like my explanation was inadequate.

And he looked at me thoughtfully and said, "Yeah, well, okay . . . I have to pee."

I would laugh at that for days after. I thought I was worthy of a feature story in *Parenting* magazine, and he was thinking about urination. Life does have a way of balancing the serious and the ridiculous. That is a very good little thing. I am thankful.

August 3rd: Happy Birthday to Me . . ..

Refuse to fall down. If you cannot refuse to fall down, refuse to stay down. If you cannot refuse to stay down, lift your heart toward heaven, and like a hungry beggar, ask that it be filled. You may be pushed down. You may be kept from rising. But no one can keep you from lifting your heart toward heaven—only you. It is in the middle of misery that so much becomes clear. The one who says nothing good came of this, is not yet listening.

~Clarissa Pinkola Estés~

At the stroke of midnight, Brendan jumped on my bed, and with one whisper to Brady, they sang "Happy Birthday" to me. It was beautiful. The tears fell freely from my eyes, and they were mixed with both a sadness of this day starting without Stephen and a happiness for the kindness that lies within the heart of my 12-year-old. He has it. It is evident, and people can see it: the goodness.

After a so-so night's sleep, I awoke as Brady was sneaking out of the room to go to his meeting, long enough to get a kiss and drift back off to sleep again. So thoughtful and kind and loving, Brady has been my one little thing for many moments in the last month.

Sitting here on a quiet morning, feeling good about staying focused on this "project," that has been a good thing. As I see the number of words I am typing continue to grow, I am feeling more confident about what I am doing. I am still not completely sure where it will lead, but I do know that this daily focus has helped me and has allowed me to keep holding the rope.

Around the house, I see "I love you" notes everywhere. Big hugs from Brendan and his obvious desire to make sure I am happy.

I pull out a handmade birthday card from my planner, one that had been given to me by Stephen and Brendan the year before. It is handmade, as I like it. I open it gently and read the words Stephen wrote:

"Thank you for being such a great mother and influence to the both of us. Every day you show us unconditional love and support, and what it's like to be part of a loving family. I hope we can make every 29th birthday as special as you do for us, every day. Love, Stephen and Brendan."

The great news for me is, because I never intend to go past 29, I will always have a birthday card from Stephen—every year. That is a big thing.

August 5th: 1812 Overture, Sunshine, and Jewel-Kissed Waves

I read and walked for miles at night along the beach, writing bad blank verse and searching endlessly for someone wonderful who would step out of the darkness and change my life. It never crossed my mind that that person could be me.

~Anna Quindlen~

I woke up early after a good night's sleep. I lie there for a long time in the quiet, thinking about my love for the ocean and feeling grateful for a few days at the beach. Coming out of a dream, the mornings are still the time when my soul is most peaceful. A rested mind, I am better able to put things in perspective. As the day wanes on, I find that fatigue brings out the highs and lows of my emotions, and my thoughts are more erratic and not so serene. It is good that I recognize that. I think back to when my parents died, and I was unable to recognize much of anything in my grief because of youth or denial or both.

In any case, the mornings are good. It is a great morning for a walk. And as much as my husband loves me and I love him back, I like my walks on the beach to be solitary. It is then that I am closest to my thoughts and maybe to God—when it is just me with the waves and the early morning sunlight.

I set out, baseball hat on, water, and Stephen's iPod. Oh, what comfort this little gadget has given me in the past month! A window into his soul, truly, from the music itself to how he titled his playlists. From this and from his other things I have found, I continue to get to know my son, even after his death. And I love what I am finding.

I walk the boardwalk to the seashore, and the sun is glistening on the water. Feeling good about the lack of beach-goers at this early hour, I know this is going to be a stroll that will bring me peace and allow me to gather my thoughts and strength for the day.

I turn on the iPod and select his "Classical" playlist. For anyone who is interested in experiencing the magnificence of a walk on the beach on an entirely different level, do so while listening to classical music. Listening to the "1812 Overture" while watching the pelicans dive down for fish as the sun glistens across the morning waves is simply splendid. "Canon in D" and "Ave Maria" were the closing numbers on my return to the beach house—and a fitting closing to a long dialogue I'd had with Stephen and God.

I find that I am having conversations more so than what some would call praying. As I stroll down the beach, I communicate, sometimes to Stephen and sometimes to God. I would, as I listened to each different piece, marvel at the fact that this boy was my child. His appreciation for this music makes me so proud! Some of the pieces I know he heard from my father, who had a lifelong love affair with the classics. Others were instrumental versions of songs I would sing to him. As a music student, I would sing to him in Latin and French. "Ave Maria," and one other in particular, with the melody of the "Pathetique Movement" by Beethoven, I can recall singing to him on many an occasion as I rocked him in my arms.

I wonder, as I stroll, if he remembered that and if that had been why he downloaded the piece from iTunes. Did it give him comfort? Did it remind him of his youth? Of us? My own memories of this personal moment between us only sparked when I listened to his iPod. How funny, just as The Beatles songs reminded me of an afternoon we played hooky and watched a movie. His iPod has been a gift to me.

As I continued walking, I kept thinking that I needed a sign from heaven. I was thinking about the butterflies that followed us down the road yesterday and was wanting yet another sign that both he and God were with me and that everything would be okay. I looked out over the water, sparkling as if the rarest of jewels had been sewn into the tip of each wave. The water felt cool on my bare feet, and the warm breeze blew softly over me. And I smiled, thinking that God was saying, "What more do you need Kelly? If you don't see this as a sign everything is okay and that we are with you and love you, a butterfly is probably not going to make you feel better."

How very true, Big Guy, I thought. This is some pretty good evidence; I just have to want to see it.

August 7th: Creating New Masterpieces

The wave of the future is coming and there is no fighting it.

~Anne Morrow Lindbergh~

Another day at the beach, a place that renews me and allows me to see my place in the world. I love to just sit and stare out at the ocean. It is a form of meditation. I've always been mesmerized at the repetitive motion of the ocean as the waves hit the shoreline and cleanse the palate. I sit and watch that motion for a while and wonder what I have in my own life that cleanses my palate. Do I have something that wipes away the things of the past and allows me to create a new masterpiece? No, rather, I think I get a new set of paints at certain points in my lifetime. I get a new palate of color that can make the existing painting deeper and more valuable. This is quite a new set of paints I have these days. I hope God threw in some new brushes as well.

One of the things I love to do at the beach is build sandcastles or sand creations. There is something wonderful about regressing back to the days of childhood, to immerse yourself in a task with such seriousness, even though it will be, in a few hours, washed away with the coming tide. It is funny when you think about it, as it is the same with life and what you create day to day. Nothing is permanent, and the tide and movement of life will wash away your creations as well. The tide of life naturally removes things and experiences and people from your life. All we are left with is the memory and the mark of love it leaves in our heart.

But as we do with the tide and the sandcastles, why don't we just accept the changes we are presented with as part of the cycle of life? We fight it, we complain, we grieve. We mourn what we have lost for so long. We have no ability to see what has arrived and is sitting right under our noses.

I am going to try to live my life more like the rhythm of the ocean and understand that the ebbs and flows of the coming tide will always bring both change and renewal.

Today, I am thankful for lessons from the deep.

August 9th: Deep Chats with My Husband and the Big Guy

Faith is the bird that feels the light and sings when the dawn is still dark.

~Rabindranath Tagore~

Ah, Sunday mornings. Lots to be thankful for on Sunday mornings: waking up in my own bed, the sun shining, and the quiet of the house and getting back to my writing. I always get a sense of renewal as we plan to embark on a new week. I don't know what it says about my personality, but I do enjoy the preparing. I say that, knowing that as much as I plan, I cannot plan for everything. I cannot make life go the way I want 100 percent of the time, that's for sure.

In the quiet, early hours, Brady and I take some time to talk openly and honestly about how we feel. I appreciate how truthful we are with each other. We cope with grief very differently, and it is good to have a checkpoint chat to make sure we are both moving in the same direction. I recognize my introversion and introspection may appear to others that I am shutting them out. I want to make sure he never feels that way. I also know that Brady's happy exterior does not always reveal what is going on in that head of his. I could see him laugh at a joke at the beach, but I noticed he could not bring himself to play bocce ball, a reminder of his happier times with Stephen. So, it is good for us to lay things out on the table.

Life is imperfect and messy. But I am glad I have someone like him to work through the mess.

One of the things we talk about is taking the right steps to keep ourselves in the right frame of mind. We have not always been good at self-nurturing, and we really need to take care of ourselves right now. We talk about the crutches in our lives and how we want to live without Stephen here with us physically. We talk about eliminating any negative and toxic forces that are around us, as we are no longer able to deal with it anymore. We talk about faith and our trust in God.

I am blessed. Because I know that talking about feelings must feel like a trip to the dentist for Brady. But he does it just the same, because he loves me.

This grief stuff is sure making me deep. But it is a good deep. I am thankful.

August 11th: Guidance

No man is great enough or wise enough for any of us to surrender our destiny to. The only way in which anyone can lead us is to restore to us the belief in our own guidance.

~Henry Miller~

The wheels are turning today as I go through every moment of my life with Stephen. In particular, I've been thinking about guidance. I've had a lot of people offer me guidance and advice in my life. Some was good, and some was bad. Some was requested, and some was just given to me, no matter how I protested.

As of late, I have received direction from many as I journey through grief. It has helped us so much. But I have to be truthful, there are some tidbits of wisdom that have been offered that honestly made me tilt my head to the right and just wonder. First, let's talk about the good stuff. "The Grief Lady" has been amazing and has helped us in so many ways. She has not pulled us in a certain direction but has instead allowed us to discover our own path in our own time. Through her gentle facilitation, we have found what has worked for us as a family. The self-discovery has been tremendously helpful for us, as well as her gentle reassurances that we are, in fact, normal. I wonder if everyone asks that question as much as I do. Am I normal?

But we have also received advice, opinion, and so-called guidance that is 100 percent outlandish. Let me give you some examples:

"It is never really going to get any better, and you just need to make peace with that."

"It is good and healthy to be angry, and you shouldn't deny your anger. You may be angry for the rest of your life."

"This is the worst thing anyone can go through in life, and you will never be the same. If I were in your shoes, I would wish for death."

"It is August now, and it is time to move on."

"It's time to get back to work and keep moving. It will help you."

"I know you miss your child, but you can't be like my friend, who turned their house into a shrine. I feel so uncomfortable when I visit them."

And my personal favorite from my physician, said to me during a routine visit for a renewal of a thyroid prescription. Note: I did **not** say I was depressed.

"Let's talk about Paxil and Prozac."

The list could go on and on. I know that people really did mean well, but did they think about how their messages would be received? Perhaps not. I think they struggled to find anything to say to me, and these were, perhaps, the only statements they could muster. In some ways, I would rather have something like these said to me than the silence from other acquaintances, who avoid me like I have leprosy. Now, take a moment to reflect on all of the statements, even the physician's instant assumption that because I was sad, I was depressed. A common theme emerges. People are uncomfortable with grief. They want you to move on from it, bury it, put away the photos, and just make peace with the fact it will never get better. People don't want to look at it. Society feels better if we medicate such emotions, smooth out the rough edges of life, if you will.

But we can only learn from it if we look right at it. Medicating the hurt does not make the pain go away. It numbs it. Stop taking the pills, and you are back to square one.

So, in my analysis of these off-the-wall statements, I can't help but reflect on my past and some of the wacky things I have been told, all in the name of "guidance."

One particular recollection of a lesson in guidance comes to mind today. I am back in high school, standing in the guidance counselor's room, looking with interest and excitement at the brochures for the universities in Atlantic Canada. It is scary and exciting to think about going away for higher education, as I have a lot to consider. I have Stephen, and my mind is somewhat confused as I contemplate the need for university education and the effect it will have on my parenting. On the best of days, with my youth and inexperience, I feel inadequate as a mother, watching my parents or older siblings and wondering why it seems to come so naturally to them. But in my heart, I know that becoming educated beyond this moment will be the only way for me to truly give Stephen what I know he deserves. And thankfully, I have a family that agrees with me, and both encouraged and supported me through that learning so I could give Stephen a better life.

So, I stand there eyeing all of the information. I had snuck in the room quietly, without any of my friends, feeling uncertain about this and so much more in my life. I've worked to get good grades, and I know I should be able to go to the school of my choice. But I am scared.

And as if she can read my mind and is feeding off my inner dialogue, the guidance counselor approaches. Genevieve, a small and frail woman, whose paper-thin appearance does not match her abrasive and aggressive approach in communication. She has this inherent ability to get under my skin and is just the individual you want to have in a position designed to encourage young people to reach for their dreams.

"What are you looking at, Kelly?" she asks, with a hint of something in her voice I cannot quite place but know it is not genuine curiosity or kindness.

"I'm looking at the brochures for school. My mom and dad wanted me to bring them home so we could read about the different options."

And then it happened. And although it was well over 20 years ago, I can remember it like it was yesterday.

"Kelly, you need to be realistic. University is not for someone like *you*."

Her words hit me like a sledgehammer in the chest, and I felt the lump grow instantaneously in my throat.

"You need to take care of your child, and you can't do what everyone else is doing anymore."

"But this is how I will take care of my child—by becoming educated. And I've already talked about it with my mom, and . . ." My words were cut off mid-sentence, as she interjected with her confident conclusion.

"Kelly, your life has a plan now, and you should not think you will be able to do this," she said. She was positive in her appraisal of my situation, although I do believe it was the first one-on-one conversation I'd had with the woman. She did not know me, my family support system. She did not know my personal ambition. She certainly did not know my love for Stephen.

And although I was raised to be a respectful girl, I could feel the lava bubbling up from within me, and I knew I could not stop it.

"You can't tell me what I can and can't do. You don't know me. I will see you in 10 years!" I said emphatically. Typing the words makes it appear as if I had control over my emotions, but the truth is, my voice was at least two octaves higher than usual, and my neck was blotchy. My neck looks like a road map in times of conflict, with blotches showing up in an instant. It bears a resemblance to a map of Europe.

And with that, I turned on my heel and walked out of the room, never to speak with her again. In fact, I ignored her, even when she spoke to me directly. I suppose I could have had issues with treating a teacher like that, but for some reason, she had made the smart decision not to address it.

Ten years later, I thought about her. I was educated and working in a great position and giving Stephen the life he deserved, and she came to mind, one day, out of the blue.

Guidance

The very word brings me back to that day. And it is a good thing to remember. For with this trip down memory lane, I am reminded that the best guidance for your own life can only truly come from you—and the Big Guy upstairs, of course.

You are the only one who understands all of the moving parts of your life, your inner strength that no one else can see but you know exists. You can listen to different points of view, of course, but you need to find out how to tap into the kind of guidance that you can rely on 100 percent of the time.

That internal guidance comes from becoming quiet and still. Quiet the voices, both outside and inside your head. Become still and release the need for constant motion. Trust your gut. Talk to God. And then wait. Sometimes, we veer off in the wrong direction because we are not patient enough to wait for the answer.

And as I have found, the answers will come.

Now, if I could figure out how to put that in every school counseling room in every school, the future of the world would be bright indeed.

I am thankful.

August 12th: The Blubbering Driver

I find the great thing in this world is not so much where we stand, as in what direction we are moving: To reach the port of heaven, we must sail sometimes with the wind and sometimes against it, but we must sail, and not drift, nor lie at anchor.

~Oliver Wendell Holmes~

Wow, I've been holding a lot inside. Because this morning, it appears that I have burst. Driving to hockey camp, Brendan and I were quietly chatting. And he asked, "Do you think Stephen knew what was going to happen to him?"

And I did not have an answer. For years, I have wondered that same question about my dad's heart attack. Always keeping his keys secure and his belongings safe, he left his full set of keys in the mailbox on the morning he collapsed. Days before that, he had a weird conversation with me about the family home and his will. It kind of shocked me to think that Brendan had those same feelings and similar questions. I did not know how to answer, only to say I did not think so but did not know. After dropping Brendan off at hockey camp, I pulled out of the Ice House parking lot, and the tears in my eyes began to flow and then actually shot from my eyes like a dam bursting. By the time I started to drive down the road, in morning traffic, I was openly sobbing, collapsing with a grief that overwhelmed me, encompassed me, enveloped the car, and made it difficult for me to breathe.

Note to self: Start carrying tissues, and always have sunglasses within arm's reach. I just can't explain it, because I like to think I am a smart person. But since this happened, I cannot, for the life of me, remember to put some tissues in my purse. I am a grown woman who has been using her sleeve for more than a month now.

I did not make direct eye contact with the people next to me in morning traffic. But I could feel their eyes on me as I sobbed, mouth open with my head kind of hung over the steering wheel, waiting for the light to turn green. Even through my tears, I could imagine that they were surmising the reason for my waterworks. Perhaps I had just found out my husband was leaving, the dog ran away, or, in this culture, my Botox appointment had been cancelled. I just kept looking forward. That is what I do. I keep looking forward, whether it is to hide from onlookers or to get through a trial in life. Because really, what is the alternative?

So, where is the good thing in this? I suppose, after some reflection, it is the fact that I am letting it out. I am letting my tears cleanse my soul, to wash away some of the hurt. Instead of looking away from all of this, I am looking at it. I am realizing that for me to come out on the other side, with my lessons in my pocket, I must grieve. I must face the reality that my precious little baby is no longer here. He is not away at school or at work or visiting in Canada. He is gone.

I am thankful that I hurt. Because through the hurt, I am taking from this that I need to become a more compassionate human being. I am thankful for the pain, because it is much like an emotional GPS, and it is taking me on a journey through Stephen's life and my own. Through the pain of this voyage, I am writing and capturing whatever I can before the ache subsides, and things like laundry and bills and life numb the hurt and make me forget all these lessons.

August 15th: It's a Beautiful Day in the Neighborhood

Let us be grateful to people who make us happy; they are the charming gardeners who make our souls blossom.

~Marcel Proust~

From a distance, I can look like I am doing okay. Up close, you can see all the cracks. And lately, I am like a piece of fine China that was dropped on the floor and then stepped on by an elephant. I could crumble to dust at any moment.

So, when I venture outside of the four walls of my home, when I'm in the yard or at the grocery store, I keep to myself. I smile, I wave, but I keep my distance and never attempt to start a conversation.

When you lose someone you love more than life itself, you simply ache. You think about the times you will no longer have with them, occasions like graduation from college, weddings, and grandchildren.

But when you lose someone tragically and suddenly, you think about more than the lost moments of the future. You think, over and over, about the final moments of that person's life. You wonder what they felt—if they hurt, suffered, felt hopeless or alone. I have the same recurring questions cycling in my mind, and I have no answers on the horizon.

So, I keep my distance. Because when I am far away, you can't see that I am about to implode like a well-planned demolition of a high rise in some far-off city. You can't see me literally gritting my teeth, trying to hold back the floodgates of emotion. From a distance, it's a beautiful day in the neighborhood.

But today, I was brave. I walked out the front door and down the driveway to join my husband as he talked with our neighbor Mike. Strong, resilient Kelly.

Until I opened my mouth.

It was the most amazing thing. Anything I tried to say came out with buckets of tears and sobs.

Perhaps I should have exited stage right and quickly sprinted for the house. Instead, I went with it. I accepted this was where I was, and I talked to him through the tears. It felt good to tell him about the outpouring of love we had experienced, to tell him about Stephen. It felt good to speak to him about our faith and our "conversation with God" since Stephen's death. And here I was, this private girl who always walked her path alone when it came to emotional hardship, standing in her driveway bawling her eyes out, waving to the neighbors as they drove by, tears running down my face. Either I really have finally figured it out or I've finally lost it.

It felt really good. I was proud of myself, as it was a huge step in my healing. And when we talked about faith, Mike made the greatest suggestion. He said he sometimes suggests that people write letters to themselves from God to answer the question, "What would God say to me?" He explained that if we believe that the Holy Spirit is in all of our hearts, we are qualified to write that letter. And sometimes it can really help.

Could I do that? Was I ready?

I am nervous about the morning. We are driving to Raleigh to get Stephen's belongings. They have been in storage since the end of the semester, and we are meeting his friends to pack them up.

Today I am thankful for going with the flow of my tears and knowing I will get another glimpse into Stephen's life tomorrow.

August 16th: Well-Packed Storage Unit, My Own Phoenix Process, the Love of College Boys, and Brendan's Need for Answers

Only when we are no longer afraid do we begin to live in every experience, painful or joyous, to live in gratitude for every moment, to live abundantly.

~Dorothy Thompson~

We awake early on this Sunday morning. I sit on the edge of the bed, again. I stare at the bags, again. *Good morning, bags. How are you? The same? That's terrific. Oh, and me? Slightly short of breath and anxious. Why, you ask? Well, my husband and I are driving up to collect my dead son's things from a storage unit, and I'm not really sure if I can emotionally handle it. You know, not feeling like I want to have my heart broken all over again.* Tears wash the sleep from my eyes.

I stare at the bag for another little while, thinking that later today, there will be other bags and boxes I will have difficulty moving or unpacking, as if they have been nailed to the floor. But time keeps moving, and we can't just leave the stuff up there.

My husband, who would do anything to protect me, asks me one more time if I really want to do this. He has said he could go without me, but I want to be there. It is much like the knapsack on the floor; I need to see this storage unit. I remember talking to Stephen that day as he and his friend Phil were moving their things in there for the summer. He and I laughed together as he described them piling their belongings into the unit. I had to see it for myself, as he had touched these things. He had piled all of his stuff in there, in anticipation of his senior year at college. He talked to me about this being the last time he would have to move this stuff, and we joked, as we knew the majority of the things he had moved from place to place in his college years would be ready for the trash by graduation. He was, after all, a boy living with boys.

So, although I appreciated Brady's valiant efforts to protect me from the pain, I knew that experiencing the pain was part of it. And I also knew that if I did not go, I would regret it. No regrets.

Brady and I had a quiet drive to Raleigh, where we chatted—about Stephen, the days, memories. It was tough, and our conversation was a little tentative, at best. It was as if we could not completely exhale in anticipation of the day. I had many thoughts about what we would find in the storage unit. I hoped for many things, although I could not articulate exactly what. I suppose in a perfect world, I would love to find a letter, laying out his entire life and feelings, written to me to explain it all in the case of his untimely death. "In case of emergency, break glass and read letter." Not quite realistic.

We arrived at the storage unit with two sets of keys, hoping that one of those sets had the key to the lock on the door. Stephen had the only key. And as if he was with us—and I think he was—the first key worked, and the lock clicked open with ease.

We stood there for a moment, pausing, knowing that when the metal door clicked open, we would receive another wallop in the face from reality. I wish reality would stop smacking me. My cheeks are flushed and burning these days from the sting of life.

Brady pushed the metal door up, and we gazed inside at the most amazing packing job. Items were precariously balanced in a way that could only have been completed by two 20-something-year-old boys who just wanted to get stuff in there so the summer could begin. Stephen was always a great person for packing things. I suppose it came from the numerous moves we made—or the numerous hockey trips. Goalie gear is not small, and sometimes, we were hard pressed to find a cubic centimeter of free space in the vehicle. He was brilliant at consolidating a large amount of "stuff," organizing it in a way that only he could. And disassembling the masterpiece when you arrived at your destination was no simple undertaking. In many cases, he would have to take the lead, as the process of unpacking was as precarious as cutting the wires on a bomb or playing a life-sized version of Jenga. One wrong move and you would be found under a mound of smelly hockey gear and dirty laundry after a long weekend of travel.

The storage unit was no different, and I could not help but smile at the sheer number of personal effects that had been crammed into the ridiculously small space. Boxes and furniture were balanced at angles that any master mathematician would want to study. It was Stephen.

His friends Phil and Ben arrived shortly after we opened the unit, and we hugged. But we also shuffled our feet, looked to the ground periodically, and made small talk. It was great to see them, but there was an unspoken hurt that hovered over all of us, as the person whom we really wanted to unpack this stuff was not here. Speaking briefly, they quickly got to work, removing items with care, and separating out Stephen's belongings from the pile.

We knew it would take several trips to get it all out and delivered, so Brady offered to make the trips with the boys, and I decided to stay at the storage unit and continue to go through some things.

Being alone there, it was as if he was sitting with me, awaiting the return of Brady and the boys. I quietly went from box to box, looking inside, assessing the contents. But I could not do that for long. I sat in his desk chair with the pink flowered seat cushion, letting the late morning sunshine down on me. I cried a little as I pushed myself around the parking lot of the storage facility in an office chair with a pink flowered seat cushion. I wondered for a moment if anyone could be watching this woman, bawling her eyes out, pushing herself around on a wheeled office chair. Then I cried a little more. It was so hard. I closed my eyes and wished for this all to be erased, to go back to July 3rd, and to change the course of history. I would not be here in the hot sun waiting to pack up his belongings. Perhaps we would be helping him move into his new apartment, laughing and joking and feeding off his excitement as he entered his senior year. We would help as we had last year, and we would take him to lunch, hug him lots, slip him some money, and then let him get back to his life. But not this year. This year, we were here—but only to pick up the remaining pieces of his life and bring them home. There was no level of anticipation in that task, just plain old sadness.

I can feel him. I can feel his spirit and his love all around me. I look around and expect for some reason to see a butterfly, but it is not there. But he is. I don't need the confirmation of the butterfly, as he is with me. And his presence is not much different than when he was alive. It is quiet, as we never really needed a lot of words. And the moment is filled with so much love.

I decided to read a little of my book to pass the time. I thought it would be a better option, rather than to continue to touch his things and have the boys return and find me, collapsed with grief, clutching onto a pair of his socks, and crying outside a storage unit. I am reading some great books, and this one in particular has been tremendously helpful. The book is titled *Broken Open: How Difficult Times Can Help Us Grow* by Elizabeth Lesser. It covers something that I have been fascinated with for most of my life: resilience. Elizabeth describes moments in life as the "Phoenix Process," or positive life change that can emerge from exceedingly difficult life events. Examples that are used relate to divorce, the loss of a child, or suffering a terminal illness.

The topics resonate with me, and I really do feel as if I've been broken open. In fact, it is a term I've used to describe how I feel before I even found this book.

And as I read about the stories of others and how they came through their own Phoenix Process, I realize that this has not been the first one for me. I have, in fact, had a sequence of these life-changing events that have affected how I live, parent, and relate to others. And as bad as they were at the time, I cannot deny the obvious truth: I am a better person because of them.

So, the most logical conclusion would be that I will become an improved person because of this too. That is a hard pill to swallow, but somehow, I know this is accurate. I wish I could have had this transformation in my thinking, in my very soul, without the loss, without the agony.

As we merge onto the main interstate to drive home after a long and emotional day, we are all quiet, with the reality of the situation sinking in. This was the last piece of him we had to collect. Now, the only job left is for us to figure how to live this new life of ours. We notice other vehicles heading towards Raleigh, loaded down, parents bringing their excited children to university, anxious to start their new adventure. I can imagine the electric feeling in those automobiles—the child, excited about the new beginning, and the parents' bittersweet emotions as their babies take their next steps in life. I watch as, one after the other, they drive towards the city, taking their kids to school. I watch, and I quietly weep as we drive away from the city to take the last pieces of Stephen home.

It was rough, I cannot lie.

We finally reach home and quickly unload everything from the truck. After a quick survey of the now full garage, we head inside the house. I am drained.

And then Brendan starts. He asks quietly at first and then more emphatically if he can go and look at the stuff. I explain that we are tired, and let's wait. He nods but 15 minutes later is back, asking the question from a different angle. Okay, I get it. And no matter how tired I am, I know he needs to do this.

So, out we go. Brendan approaches his exploration with wild abandon, pulling open boxes and ripping out the contents. It makes me a little short of breath, as my approach with Stephen's things has been a little different. I open things slowly, inspect not only the contents but how they were packed, drinking up every detail. Brendan, however, appears to be on his own personal mission. He is looking for something, something specific. And although I am uncomfortable as he rips open the boxes, I let him go. He needs this, to find a connection, just as much as I do but in a different way. After a few boxes, he finds it. An *ESPN* magazine that he and Stephen had talked about, with a cover story on Carey Price, the Montreal Canadiens ice hockey goalie, and a t-shirt. And as if this was enough to hold onto for now, he smiles and says that this is good. He goes off into the house, and I linger, peeking inside the open boxes at the contents. And beneath a stack of school papers, there it is. A leather-bound journal. I quickly tuck it away in the basket of laundry and take it upstairs. I need to have it to myself at first.

The entries are erratic and beautiful and emotional. They paint a picture of a boy growing into a man. In his notes, he was working through some important issues—things like love, his parents' divorce, the relationship with his dad, and girls. And then I find the final entry. April 19, 2009. He had not written in the book for some time, and you can see the difference. His first entry was dripping with youth-filled angst. This final entry was made by a man, a wonderful and centered man who was excited about the opportunities that lay before him.

He began by joking about his previous entries and their relationship to his raging hormones. I smiled and had to agree. He went on to give a summary of where things were going in his life. He mentioned Brady and I, his wonderful relationship with Brendan, his love life, and his future. And what no iPod, piece of clothing, or chat with a friend could tell me, he told me all on his own. He told me he was happy.

I buried my head in my pillow and just let it all out. I was so thankful to be able to read his own words and understand he was really happy. But at the same time, I could not help but feel an overwhelming sadness that he had been taken away so soon. His final written words had said that he was excited to see what life had in store for him and that he would write more at the end of the summer.

So, what am I grateful for on this tough day? His friends, who love in a way I did not expect from college boys. My husband, who is my rock, and Brendan, who is braver than me, looking directly into the sadness, showing me I can too.

And Stephen. As I have written, I wonder if people know, have some unconscious understanding about their end of days.

Whatever your motivation, your words comfort me. They confirm your happiness, and that somehow makes me feel like I did my job as your mother. They confirm your love—for life and for others. They confirm you were exactly whom I knew you to be, and knowing that we really were that close does comfort me.

So, now we have all your things with us. I am thankful not for the things. Rather, I am most thankful for the newfound knowledge. It is not the things. We've had you right with us in our hearts all along.

August 17th: There is No Ceiling in Our House

If I had my child to raise all over again, I'd build self-esteem first, and the house later.
I'd fingerpaint more, and point the finger less.
I would do less correcting and more connecting.

I'd take my eyes off my watch, and watch with my eyes.

I would care to know less and know to care more.
I'd take more hikes and fly more kites.

I'd stop playing serious, and seriously play.
I would run through more fields and gaze at more stars.
I'd do more hugging and less tugging.

I'd see the oak tree in the acorn more often.

I would be firm less often, and affirm much more.

I'd model less about the love of power,

And more about the power of love.
~Diane Loomans~

I've always seen parenting as a job that is a combination of cheerleading, love, and mystic guidance. It is my business to build my child up, because let's face it: the world will beat you down at times. You have to train yourself and your children to know that your home is always a haven where, without a doubt, everyone loves you without condition. Imagine if every home and parent tried that for a year. How would the world change? How would the world be different if all of the children walked out their front doors in the morning feeling loved and confident in their gifts and knowing that at the end of the day, they had a safe place to which they could return?

I know that some would say you should paint a realistic picture for your child to help shield them from disappointment. But you know what? You can't shelter your child from disappointment, no matter how hard you try. It is there, and it is part of life just like death is. If you could, I would have been able to shield Brendan from July 4th, 2009. But I could not. It comes, we deal with it, and we figure out how we use it to make us stronger and more compassionate people.

So, rather than buffer children from disappointment, why not teach them how to deal with it? Why not give them a strong sense of self by telling them you think they are the best thing since sliced bread, and here are the 182 reasons why? Then, when disappointment comes, they will see it is a disappointment for one thing, one part of their life, not *all* of their life. What about the value of raising resilient children?

Maybe I am completely off target, but I think we only get to do this once, so why not dream big? Why not believe that you can do anything you set your mind to and then see what happens? Why not build a solid foundation for your child's house instead of building the ceiling first?

Thinking about this brings up a memory of Stephen not accepting limitations.

He had applied to NC State. Having spent his first year at a community college in Charlotte, North Carolina, he was now ready to get going. He attended the college to prepare, take the SAT, and get used to this new country. In our first year here, I was thankful he was home with me and not away. Now, looking back, I am blessed that he was slow to start with his university education. I had 2 extra years with him at home that I now know were a gift.

He was on the Dean's List at the college. So, when we applied to NC State, we simply assumed it was just a matter of time before we received his letter of acceptance. And when the letter arrived, Stephen was smiling as he opened it. But it was not a letter of admission. It was a letter indicating he did not meet the criteria for a transfer student and would need an additional 6 credits. *Please try again next time.*

The look on his face broke my heart. He had worked so hard and had been so diligent in his planning. He had already been in touch with the hockey coach at NC State. But now, it appeared it was over. He showed me the letter, and I read it carefully.

After some reflection, I looked up and said, "Stephen, we don't accept this. This is not saying they don't want you. This is saying you need some extra courses to be admitted. There is a difference. I will call them and ask them what we can do."

He looked anxious but slightly relieved. We had always found solutions in the past for whatever came up, and I think he was glad to see this circumstance would be no different.

I called the school and spoke with the most wonderful person in the admissions office. She explained that yes, he did need the courses to qualify as a transfer student, but if he could get those courses, he would be admitted because his grades were terrific. I asked her to put a hold on his application and assured her he would have the grades by her deadline of mid-July.

I hung up the phone feeling encouraged but knew this would mean Stephen would have to take an insane number of courses in the compressed spring semester in order to make this happen. I talked to him about it, explaining that it would mean he would have to work constantly for the next three months if he wanted this. But if he did want it, he could have it.

He needed it, and he worked nonstop for that semester, getting all As and Bs. And as promised, the admissions department processed the application, and he was ready to go for the fall. At the end of the process, I actually sent the admissions counselor flowers. She had been so professional and so good at her job, and she had gone above and beyond for us. Do you know why? Because we asked her to, because we did not take no for an answer.

I think back on that now and all that he had done to make it happen in his life, and I am amazed. At the time, it just seemed like it was the thing to do.

That's my one little thing for the day. I realize that my job as a parent is to be "the keeper of the dream." Sounds like I should be part of some sort of trilogy of stories about fairies and monsters but not quite so dramatic. Rather, it is simple. I am thankful because I now know, by reflections on my life with Stephen, how important it is to encourage your children to dream big and not accept no for an answer in life. And coupled with that, when things don't work out—and sometimes that will happen—you show them how to bounce back. I am thankful that even though we feel a little beaten up, I am continuing to parent Brendan with that same sense of resilience.

August 19th: I-I-I-I-I-I A-A-A-A-M-M-M-M Astro Boy!!!!!

Up, Up and Away!

~Superman~

I am thinking about superheroes today. With Brendan back at school, I took some time this morning to quietly look through Stephen's things. While removing boxes from his bedroom closet, I came across a board game and a figurine that made me laugh out loud and then cry. Astro Boy. A few years back, Brady and I found these treasures on a back shelf at some store, and knew we had to have them. And on Christmas morning, Stephen laughed with a full and rich guffaw as these two simple and goofy presents gave him a trip down memory lane.

You see, Stephen was obsessed with Astro Boy. No, obsession is an incorrect description. He wanted to *BE* Astro Boy. For a period of time between ages three and four, I believe he thought he *WAS* Astro Boy. One of his favorite cartoons, he would watch and then imitate the boy hero with rockets for feet and a heart of gold. He really thought he could do it, become this superhero and save the world.

It was beautiful to watch him, his innocence, and his unwavering belief that he could do it. He could be a superhero.

Dressed for the day with pants and a shirt and socks, he would disappear. Minutes later, he would saunter out into the hallway with nothing on but his briefs and his blue rubber boots. This was his superhero outfit, and it closely resembled the uniform of his idol, Astro Boy. He would run into the room and then jump into the air. And when his feet hit the ground, he would have his hands on his hips—as any crusader should—and would announce in a loud and authoritative voice,

"I AM ASTRO BOY!!"

His enthusiasm for the role was hilarious. So was the fact that for a period of time, it was difficult for me and my family to keep him dressed.

And although he did not have rockets in his feet or a laser in his behind, I think Stephen was a superhero just like Astro Boy. He was kind and looked out for others and had people's best interests at heart. He had all of the characteristics of a comic book hero, without the cape or superpowers. At least that is how I see it.

Perhaps that is what we should all be doing with our children: nurturing the superhero within. Cultivate those characteristics that make them stand out in a crowd and stand up for what is right. Superheroes may bend, but they don't break. They may not win every battle, but they persevere and never lose sight of what is important, good, and just. With superheroes, they show us there is always a next time, another time to get up and dust ourselves off and try again.

Later in the day, I wait for the school bus with nervous anticipation. And as I look at his face as he is walking towards me, Brendan smiles the biggest grin I've seen in weeks. He did it! He came back happy. Thank you, thank you, and thank you.

Today I am thankful for successful first days. I am thankful for happy memories and how many of them I have stored away.

And I am thankful for superheroes.

August 20th: The Face of Adversity, the Roots Knapsack, and the Education of Kelly

Pain is inevitable. Suffering is optional.

~Author Unknown~

People use standard phases in times of trouble, strife, and challenge. These are things that can inspire or commiserate, comfort or irritate.

One of the things I can recall reading and hearing more than once since July 4th is this phrase:

"In the face of adversity"

In the written word, you hear this phrase in the description of someone who faced insurmountable odds. Faced with adversity, they . . . and so the story goes. In the spoken word, I have had well-meaning people tell me that you learn about yourself in the face of adversity. I believe that to be true.

In finding my little thing for the day, I have been thinking about "the face of adversity." In my little play on words, I have been imagining just what the face of adversity would, in fact, look like. In my youth, I would probably say the face of adversity looked like the people who hurt me, the people who were mean to me or made fun of me. But as I have aged, like a good red wine, I have more character, more depth—and yes, I have a fuller body. I understand that the people who have hurt me are a part of the journey and always leave me with a lesson to take from the experience.

I also probably would have said that the face of adversity was me, my reflection in the mirror. As I looked upon the changing landscape of my appearance, I could say that adversity was mapped across my cheeks, in the darkness beneath my eyes, the crow's feet or frown lines. But again, I see that as a youthful interpretation. Things happen in life, but they do not define you or anyone else for that matter, unless you let them.

Today, after having time in this reflective state of heartache, I believe I can say what the face of adversity looks like. I can tell you, based on the recent loss of my child and every other difficult time I have had along the way. All of those events, with their pain, have given me insight.

And as I see it, the face of adversity is one of a gentle teacher. She is quiet, and she looks towards you, feeling empathetic for the hurt that is in your life. I think we should look gently into the eyes of adversity and see that there is love and compassion. She has old and knowing eyes, and she has seen pain like yours before—many times. She understands. She has cried with me, tears for the loss of an extraordinary human being.

In her eyes, her laugh lines and frown lines, there is understanding. There is a knowing. In her face, if you are brave enough to look at her, you can see what is profoundly important, and she will reveal to you a courage within you that you cannot see without her help.

I think we should understand that even if adversity is looking upon us right now, she will turn her head and looks towards others as well. We are not alone, and she looks upon everyone from time to time in life. No one lives without a visit from her.

I have been reading ferociously since July 4th. I have been writing with a passion that I have never had before. It is as if I have been given a secret message from my teacher Adversity, and I am trying to get it all down before I forget. I think we should stop looking at the "face of adversity" in much the same way we look at a cartoon Halloween image of the Grim Reaper or a scary monster. I believe we need to look at her as a friend who brings with her a bag of wisdom. She loves us, and she is with us to comfort us.

She is beautiful in her own way, and within her eyes, you can see the real story of what you have lost, and you can learn all that you need to know to move forward. But if you want to gain the insight that she offers, you must be brave enough to look at your reality with the hope of making peace with it.

We must learn that visits from adversity are much like life and death itself. It is part of our existence and is not something to fight or resist. We are not in control of the calendar or the agenda; it is set by something larger than ourselves.

Seeing "her" for the beautiful instructor she is has changed me forever. It has allowed me to take good from this situation rather than shut my heart down and become bitter. It has allowed me to understand and see that there is so much love surrounding me. It has encouraged me to become a better parent, to take all the lessons and work at becoming more of who I was designed to be. It has allowed me to understand what the phrase "God's Grace" means. Looking at her and taking her hand gave me strength and grace I never knew existed.

She is not someone you want to visit you often. But when she does—and she will—we all need to stop and make ourselves still and know that she loves us, she feels our pain, and she has something to teach us, something that will help us go on and live again, better than we were living before.

So, I am thankful today for what adversity is teaching me about appreciating life.

And moving on from the deep stuff, I am thankful for another important thing today.

Ta-ta-ta dah! (Trumpet sounds of announcement)

I removed the bags from the floor of my bedroom.

It was time. I knew that. So, this morning, I looked down at them and gently explained, "I love you. And you've really been there for me, taught me so much. But it's time we move on and go our separate ways. I will always hold you in my heart, maybe take you on some hockey trips, but we can't go on this way any longer. But let's still be friends."

I joke as I write this, but honestly, it was tough. I picked the bags up off the floor and put them on my bed. I looked at them for a long time; I took out some of the things and put them back. I smelled his t-shirts. I held my breath, which really did not do me any good.

And then I carried them out of the room as I cried. I took them down the hall, opened the door to Stephen's room, and laid the bags on his bed. I did not unpack them. I just dropped them off and closed the door.

I returned to my room and exhaled. It was time. It was time to take the next step. It was time to remove the 49 days' worth of dust from that spot on the floor. Okay, from the rest of the floor too. It was time to open the blinds and let the sun in and clean the room.

So, today, I am thankful for my two teachers: Adversity and the Roots Knapsack. Through them, I have been presented with both memories and lessons. I have been given opportunities to understand the mysteries and glories of life—even through pain.

I am thankful.

August 21st: Don't Worry, He Can Take It

People are like stained-glass windows. They sparkle and shine when the sun is out, but when the darkness sets in, their true beauty is revealed only if there is light from within.

~Elizabeth Kübler-Ross~

This is hard work. Most days, as I try to move through the world, I feel like I am wearing lead boots, a lead jacket, and have 50 pounds of rocks in my pockets. The physical ache in my chest is exhausting, and my jaw hurts from clenching it. I hold it tight to prevent myself from falling apart. I know I've committed to this gratitude thing, but don't kid yourself. It still hurts.

But one of the curious things I've noticed is people assume I am mad at God. When people ask how I'm doing, I say I am working through this, and I've been having a conversation with the Big Guy. And there first response to me is, "Don't worry, He can take it."

Take what? I'm not mad at God.

I find that curious, that the immediate assumption would be that I am calling the Big Guy out for what has happened in my life. People immediately assume that I am working through the bitterness and the anger, and I honestly am not.

I believe that they assume this standpoint because we, as human beings, rarely approach times of hardship with an open heart of gratitude. We become angry and upset and feel once again the world has done us wrong. We stamp our feet and cry out. We feel entitled to feel that way for what we have lost. We are focused on the misconception that our life is supposed to be all sunshine and roses. That is an illusion that we have created, that we have bought into as we watch the weekly shows displaying reality as something that is perfection—in situation, in body size, in looks, in attainment of material possessions. All of it. We have numbed ourselves from what is real. And real life sometimes hurts. And hurt can be our greatest teacher if we decide to sit ourselves down and absorb the lesson.

If I focused on the loss in this situation, I would be so angry, "going Irish" all over God right about now. But through the shift in my thinking to consciously focusing on gratitude, I have been able to remove the anger and the bitterness from the process of my grief.

Do I have moments where, for an instant, I feel like I picked the short straw in life? Yes, I am only human. But, for the other 98 percent of the time, I am able to focus on what is good in my life, what good we can take from Stephen's life instead of what we have lost.

So, my little thing for today? My outlook on life. I am proud of myself, and I think Stephen would be proud of me as well. It is my decision to grieve in this way that allows me to keep breathing, to keep going, to keep parenting Brendan, and to keep being a partner to Brady. It is allowing me to record this entire journey. And it is changing my life, without a doubt. Sounds like a massive thing to me.

August 22nd: Two Goalies in the Crease

When life takes the wind out of your sails, it is to test you at the oars.

~Robert Breault~

Today, Brendan has his big kick-off weekend for hockey, so the house is filled with nervous anticipation. For Brendan, this is a big step, to get back out on the ice, and Brady and I are so proud of him and how hard he has worked to get here. As the tryouts were approaching in the spring, he worked out every day. He went to camps, and he would do dry land training with Stephen.

Those are happy memories for Brendan leading up to this moment, but I also know it is bittersweet, as he knows Stephen's not here, physically at least, to watch him play.

Yes, today is different. Stephen is not here, and we have had quiet conversations about it. Brendan's questions and comments about Stephen and grief are random and spurt out of his mouth when you least expect it. Last week, he posed a question to me about Stephen's remains as we were standing in the checkout line at Target. I actually love that about him, but I think the cashier was horrified. I feel truly blessed that we are talking; we are working it out, even if it is not pretty as we do so.

So, this morning, as he prepares, he is laying out his equipment, making sure his skates and stick are ready to go, getting the right socks. And as I type this, I know it does not sound like this is a big deal. But to truly understand the ritualistic tendencies involved in the preparation process, you would need to be here, to be the mother of a goalie. It is all about doing the same things in the same way, wearing the same socks, drinking the same beverage, listening to the same music as we drive to the arena.

They say that if you want to be a really great goalie, you have to be a little "off," a little crazy. I don't know about that, but you do have to march to your own drum. Anyone who willingly stands in the cold waiting and wanting to be hit by a frozen hard black disc has to be a truly unique individual. I wonder what that says about me— I produced two goalies.

And in between the prep work, he stops here and there and asks a question. His words tell me he has been thinking about Stephen all morning.

"Do you think he would be proud of me?" he asks.

I, of course, know he was proud of Brendan before he made this team, and he was so excited when Brendan heard that he had, in fact, been selected back in June. I tell him so, but my words always seem to fall short, because I am the wrong person telling him. I am not Stephen.

"Do you think he is with me?" Big question for a little boy. Big question for a mom, one I have been contemplating myself.

"Yes, I think he is with you. I think he is with all of us, in our hearts and watching over us." I type this, having no idea what the experts would say about presenting the information to my child in this way. Nor do I care. I feel flawed in how I am helping him sometimes, but I am trying my best. When I don't know an answer, I tell him. And I do believe Stephen is with us every day. I believe he is with others he loved as well.

And then, Brendan gives me confirmation that I said what he needed to hear. He smiles the biggest smile, and we joke about how an extra blocker and glove in the net is going to be helpful.

I am thankful.

The day goes great for Brendan and for us too. It is truly my big trip outside, back in the world, for the entire day and not just a few minutes at a time. I was apprehensive about it; I still find myself at a loss for words, and when I do have the words, I also have the lump in my throat when I begin to speak. I wonder if I can do this, be around people who are happy and cheerful, who have lives that are still normal. I am also apprehensive about the safety of Brendan on the ice. I think about the hit to the chest Stephen took, and I cannot deny I worry about my remaining son. But Stephen was hit thousands of times before, and it was just something that happened. It was his time. I cannot put Brendan in a bubble. He has to live and live large, because we know how short and fleeting our time here can be. And just as I told Brendan that Stephen is with us, maybe I need to tell myself that very same thing. Perhaps I can ask him to use his blocker and glove to save me from some things as well, even if those things are just fearful thoughts.

I am thankful. Our family is brave as we step back into life, and we are surrounded by people who love us. And of course, we have our own special goalie in our crease.

August 23rd: You've Got Mail

*I know God will not give me anything I can't handle. I just wish that He
didn't trust me so much.*

~Mother Teresa~

Today is a good day. I finished my "Letter from God." Each day, as
suggested to me by our neighbor and friend, I have been quietly
working on what I feel God would say to me.

The process of writing this has been remarkable and life changing. I
have not only shed tears through the writing, but I have also
howled with sadness. I have made sure to only work on this when
Brendan was out of the house. Although I am open and honest
about my sadness and I show him my tears, I don't think he would
be prepared for the display.

Brady, as I worked on this, periodically peaked around the corner of
the office door after hearing my howls and sobs and would ask, "Is
everything okay in here?" He is so gentle and kind to me, and his
support is unwavering. I usually respond through tears to tell him it
is all good.

I've written for some time about my relationship with God and my
faith since July 4th. I am thankful for it, grateful for the path I did
choose—not that I can take credit for it. I felt I was being guided,
and I also felt like there was no alternative but to surrender to God.
I type that with humility, because I know I would not have
admitted that I had surrendered to God and His will before all of
this happened. My faith was real back then, but it was a faith of
convenience, one based on tradition and family history and school
doctrine, and Irish Catholic female guilt. I will admit it. Guilt played
a part in my relationship with God.

But now, it is different. My relationship with Him has progressed. And as I walk through the valley, He is walking with me, and as the famous poem "Footprints in the Sand" says, in some places He is carrying me.

I realize now that you can't choose not to hurt, but you can choose not to suffer. I feel I am making that choice. I am choosing to embrace the hurt but not the suffering. You can also choose to see God as a loving and healing God or a punishing God.

One example in particular came from the book *When Bad Things Happen to Good People* by Harold S. Kushner. I know this is a classic, and I purchased it for that very reason. But, as I have read it, I found that not all parts resonated with me as I thought they would. However, the one piece that struck me was an excerpt inserted from another book, *The Faith and Doubt of Holocaust Survivors* by Reeve Robert Brenner: "It never occurred to me to question God's doings or lack of doings while I was an inmate of Auschwitz, although of course I understood others did . . . It never occurred to me to associate the calamity we were experiencing with God, to blame Him, or to believe in Him less or cease believing in Him at all because He didn't come to our aid. God doesn't owe us that, or anything. We owe our lives to Him."

This man, facing so much hate and anger, hanging on to life with almost no hope, never entertained turning away or against God. Even when it seemed that no one would come and that the world and God had abandoned him in his time of need, his faith remained. He never once thought to blame God for his hardship.

I find that both amazing and validating for me. Because although the two events are so vastly different, his statement is exactly how I feel about my pain. With this letter, I honestly feel the weight of my hurt lifting. I also feel that what I have written is what God would say to me or *is* saying to me. It slows a racing mind and quiets the dark thoughts. I will be thankful for this letter for many years to come and go back to it when I lose sight of the truth.

At first, I thought I would not share it here, but I've decided it is part of my journey. Here goes . . .

Dear Kelly,

I wanted to send you a little note, as I know you've been having a tough time lately. I thought a letter would be better than parting the clouds, as I know you've spent a lot of time with your own words since Stephen died. I've watched you try and work through this, and I have cried tears right along with you. Losing a child is the hardest thing. I know that, as I lost my only Son. The pain is unbearable, and it feels like a heavy robe that is weighing you down each and every day.

You need to take comfort in some things. I know you are working awfully hard on keeping the faith, and I am proud of you for that. Stephen is proud of you too. He is watching over you every single day and sees how hard you try.

Here's what I need you to know:

*Stephen is safe, and he is happy here in heaven with me. He is finally with his brother Matthew, and what a reunion that was! You always said that you thought he was searching for something, and I want you to know that he has finally found it. Matthew was with him that night, and so was I. I need you to know he was okay, and he wasn't alone. He was **never** alone.*

Stephen said to tell you he loves you dearly. He had a great life, and you were a wonderful mom. He wants you to hold on to those amazing memories. He said to remind you of how happy you all were as a family. That is rare these days, Kelly. Hold on to that, as some people live to a ripe old age and never figure out the secret of life is love. He wants you to give Brady a big hug and tell him he was so thankful for the last 4 years. What they had together was rare, and the love they shared helped him fully blossom on earth. He wants Brendan to know that he is the best brother ever and that he is always with him. They have a special bond, and that bond cannot be broken by death or anything else. Tell Brendan that Stephen is right there in the crease with him for every game and right beside him in life.

Stephen is here with his brother, your parents, your aunts and uncles, and a whole bunch of others! They welcomed him with open arms, and your mother had one of her special hugs just for him. Your dad was so happy to see him. We've all been so excited to watch him play hockey; it's quite a popular sport up here, you know. And you were right when you joked with Brendan about that thunderstorm. It was Me banging on the boards after an amazing save by your boy. Stephen was so honored to see how his NC State teammates decided to remember him—from tattoos to retiring his jersey to the memorial tournament. I, of course, was not surprised. Tell them Stephen will be watching and to show up for every game and to skate like it is the Stanley Cup final.

I have some special work for Stephen to do. I know you said you always thought he was destined for greatness, and you were right. And that greatness will be achieved by serving Me. There is a lot happening right now, and I know you can feel it. Stephen will be terrific for what I have in mind for him. And you will see him in things in your life and others as they unfold. You will smile and know he played a part. I know it is hard for you to understand now, but one day, I will explain everything. One day, this will all make sense. You know, God's plan and all that stuff. I liked the way you explained God's plan to Brendan. Stephen was a surprise, wasn't he? I love surprise parties. I am proud of you for being able to see the good in difficulty. You are allowing yourself to learn from these things, and that is what I need you to do to be the person I was thinking of when I created you. Even this situation. You will find it. I will help you. Have faith; trust in My love for you.

Your grief, it says a lot about the depth of your love for Stephen. You are hurting pretty badly. But keep reminding yourself: it is not from regret. When you reviewed your relationship, I think you know you loved him as hard as you could. He knows that too.

I am so glad you listened to Me and made the changes in your life that needed to happen. I know that right now, you are so thankful you did. You gave Stephen that once-in-a-lifetime relationship with Brady and a happy home and an opportunity to grow into an amazing man, be happier than he has ever been, have an amazing college experience, and feel the thrill of the crowd cheering for him in the net. You did that because you listened to the whisper in your ear. That was Me, by the way. Continue to listen and talk to Me. I will show you the way through this too.

The Butterflies. Yes, it's him. There was so many at the memorial because he and all of your family up here wanted to envelope you with our love. We knew how badly you were hurting, and how it was hard for you to breathe with your heart broken, open as it was. And we wanted to be there and celebrate Stephen right along with you. And all the butterflies since then — that was Stephen too. For you and for those who loved him. The one that followed you on your walk, all the butterflies on the road to the beach, the one that stayed and stayed at the pool with you, Brady, and Brendan. And the one that sat on the trunk of the oak tree as you cried on Saturday. That was Stephen saying he loved you and saying thank you for having Ross and Nate come and stay. He was really happy that you told Ross your thoughts about what happened that day. I know Ross did not say much, but it gave him a lot of comfort and will help him move on. He has carried a heavy load since then, and we need to help lift that for him so he can have a happy life.

You are doing well with your writing. I know it is foreign to you to just let go, but it is a good thing sometimes to simply submit to something bigger than yourself. If you can't do it now, when can you, right? I also know you sometimes doubt yourself and wonder why the heck you are doing this, but please know I am guiding you. I believe that you can help yourself and maybe others by sharing your story, by sharing your lessons. I know that deep down, you know that too. Have faith in that, and trust that I have this all figured out. Keep focused on doing it for the right reasons, and I promise it will give you happiness in your heart.

I've been watching you wrestle with two issues. Don't you love my curveballs? Just kidding. I want you to know that Stephen and I are on the case with both, so keep sending love, and everything will fall into place as it should. Stephen was a smart cookie. And in the situation, you struggle with, you are right. All it would have taken was two words to make it better: **I'm sorry.** *Life is like that, you know. People build walls up against one another when two words could start the healing and fix everything. So, you need to stop carrying the burden of this unfinished business. Back in the spring, you talked about forgiveness, and that was big. It took a long time for you to forgive, and I knew it was difficult to talk to Stephen about giving people another chance when you were just learning yourself. And Kelly, he did forgive.*

So, where does that leave you? I want to tell you: I am proud of you for thinking this through.

That is strength.

You are on the right path. The path is love, Kelly. Anger never achieved anything. It never helped people learn lessons or communicate more effectively or change how a person will treat people, adults, and children. Anger closes doors, and love opens them. You know that. I know what your favorite quote is:

Forgiveness is the fragrance that the violet sheds on the heel that has crushed it.

~Mark Twain~

That's a good one, Kelly, and it's true. I may have given good old Mark some help with that one.

So, continue to think with Me on this one. But know that all of that hurt that Stephen felt over things from his past is gone now. He understands it now. I've spent some time with him, and I've explained everything.

I believe you can figure out a way to make this into a lesson, Kelly. I think you can turn this around with love and make this into something that will show you and those around you how to be better people.

I hope my words give you some comfort. I know it is hard to breathe some days, but I promise it will get better. Love the people around you and let them love you back. Keep looking for the good in life, and I promise, I will lead you to it.

I love you, and I will take care of you. Stephen loves you too and will be with you to watch over and guide you. Have faith in that, and watch for the glimpses of his love in the days to come. Watch for my blessings too, because you are My child and I love you in the same way that you love Stephen.

And finally, have faith that the love that you and Stephen both shared cannot be diminished by the passage from life to death. You will one day see that he was just in another room in My house of love, waiting to give you one of his famous hugs.

Love and Peace,

God

August 25th: Moving On? No. Moving Forward? No. Moving In . .

Our deepest fear is not that we are inadequate. Our deepest fear is that we are powerful beyond measure. It is our light, not our darkness, that frightens us most. We ask ourselves, "Who am I to be brilliant, gorgeous, talented, fabulous?" Actually, who are you not to be? You are a child of God. Your playing small does not serve the world. There is nothing enlightened about shrinking so that other people won't feel insecure around you. We were born to make manifest the glory of God that is within us. It's not just in some of us; it's in everyone. And as we let our own light shine, we unconsciously give other people permission to do the same. As we are liberated from our own fear, our presence automatically liberates others.

~Marianne Williamson~

Moving On

Those words keep coming up in my mind and out of the mouths of others who mean well when they phrase the passage of time in that way. Those two words are said with firmness, a suggestive tone, as if giving a verbal nudge to the receiver. *We've had enough of this now. We need to move on. You need to move on.*

I've heard those words before. When I buried one baby and took another home. When I had sleepless nights, worried about returning to school and the looks and snickers from others when I returned to school as a mom. When I had to be away from Stephen for school—no matter how right it was, it felt so wrong. When my parents died, way too soon, without seeing me fully blossom into the woman I knew I was on the inside. When I was married and embarking on a new journey. When I had to move far, far away from my home and family, with doubts and an uncertain future. When I was hurt by someone I loved so bad I could not see myself anymore and lost myself for years. When I found myself and divorced. When I quit my really, really good job and skipped out of the office, knowing I was listening to my soul. When I moved to another country and drove across the United States with my children on our "most excellent adventure." When I started fresh and gave myself another chance. When the stars and the moon aligned and God brought me to an amazing man and I fell in love. When I married that man and knew in my heart I was meant to be with him for the rest of my days. When I looked around my life and it was all so, so good, and I had to pinch myself. When I lost my son, my pride and joy, and I had to figure out how to put myself back together.

Whew! I've heard those words more than I thought. Don't tell the *Lifetime* channel about me. They will want to do a movie of the week, or a miniseries.

But for as much as I've heard and said those words, I don't think they are correct. Because moving on is not what I am doing. I can't simply move on from this, and the assumption that I could is ridiculous.

Moving forward? Yes, to a point, but it does not adequately describe the change that has happened in my life. We move forward every day, whether we like it or not.

I feel it is more like a moving *in*. Moving into my own soul, my own being, finally letting go of everything and just being me, hurt and all. Imagine, I had to be completely broken in order to do it. Life had to wallop me in order for me to let go of some of my old thought patterns, fears, and anger. Much like the quote for the day, I have held myself back in a way, for fear of what I may find behind curtain number three. But I am not afraid anymore.

Yes, moving in sounds more accurate. And now that I am finally here, I think I'll stay a while.

I am thankful today for the progress I've made and for the journey to come.

August 27th: The Grief Lady, Comfort in Words, and Perspective from Listening to the Shouting Lady

Perhaps they are not stars, but rather openings in the heaven where the love of our lost ones pours through and shines down upon us to let us know they are happy.

~Author Unknown~

Today we returned to visit "The Grief Lady." This morning's appointment is a wonderful release. I explain where I am with things, where I am with my grief. I am reduced to tears by verbalizing the words, "I am starting to feel better . . ."

Truthfully, I am not. For a moment, a blink, a heartbeat, I think that I can, but one song on the radio, one glance at a picture or memory, and I am right back to that shoreline on the lake begging for some sort of deal with God.

Talking through this helps. This is a lesson I have learned late in life. Sometimes, it is not about finding answers or solutions; sometimes, there are no immediate answers to be found to the difficult situations or questions of life. But simply letting it out is the answer.

Smiling at Brendan, I leave him in the capable hands of Dr. Clarisse and make my way to the waiting area to sit as he has his time with her. I think he needs to be able to let it out, without worrying about me and my feelings.

I sit outside, tune the radio to some classical music, and open my planner. I like gathering my thoughts, righting the ship at certain points in the day. I write a little as I sit quietly, with "Canon in D" playing in the background.

And then, through the thick hardwood of the office door next to Dr. Clarisse, I hear it. It is loud and abrasive, like fingernails on a chalk board. It is obnoxious and rude and just plain angry. It is the voice of discontent.

The classical music, although soothing, cannot drown out the complaints that echo throughout the hallway. Apparently, this woman feels that raising her voice during this session will express her opinion more emphatically. I sympathetically take a moment of silence for the counselor sitting across from her and wonder what she does to decompress after listening to a client like this one for an hour. Maybe she has a special negativity chamber that she immerses her body in for hours after a session like this one.

"Have I not done enough? I tell you, I am the one to take him to soccer and to basketball!! And what does he do? Nothing! Absolutely nothing! He sits there and says nothing. And when he gets into trouble, he does not discipline him. He lets him get away with everything!" The voice behind the door shouted.

On and on it went. There was no pause, and I wondered how this woman was breathing. And in this 20-minute litany of complaint, there was not one thing said that could be remotely considered positive. Not one thing good about the man she married or her child. I was desperately trying not to hear it, but I could not help it, it was so loud.

The kicker for me was when she asked, "Have I not taught him how to pray and be Christian?" See, this is where I don't get it. Is this *being Christian?*

This woman had a list of all the things she had done right, an extensive list of all the things she did for her family every day. And, no doubt, it was a lot of tasks and action items. But she could not, in an entire hour, find one thing that they had done for her, and she was unable to verbalize one good thing about them. She could only see what they had done wrong and how she was a victim.

For an instant, a surge rushed through my body. I shifted in my chair, prepared to pounce. What a scene I could create, bursting in the room and telling her a thing or two about what she was missing. I could say something like, "At least your child is still alive, you selfish pile of crap."

And then I exhaled. No, that is not who I am. I still felt like bursting in, if for nothing else, to save the therapist from a death due to an overexposure to negative energy. But this is what I would say:

Let me reframe this for you. Your family is not content because you are not looking for things to be content about. You are looking for all the wrong things in your life and in them, and you are finding them. You are missing the point, as your happiness can be found by simply flipping a switch in your brain.

Be grateful.

Love solves it all.

Your husband probably feels like a failure in your eyes and wants to feel like he is loved and respected by you. Show him some of that, and you may be able to meet in the middle instead of feeling like he is out to undermine you. Your child wants the same. He wants to feel like you are proud of him and that you see his goodness. Your recognition of his goodness is like sunshine to a flower, and it will allow his goodness to grow.

And let's be honest here. You want love too. Because if you felt loved, you would not be screaming so loud, announcing all of the things you do for everyone, looking for recognition. It seems like there has been a running tally in your house for way too long, so no one can show genuine gratitude anymore. If you want some of it, give some of it back, honey. Tell your family what they give to you each day. One day soon, your child will climb into a car and drive off to create a life of his own. And if you never appreciated the one he had under your roof, why would he invite you to be part of one that is independent of your rules? You only get one chance at this, sugar cakes. Wake the heck up!

I realize I don't know the entire story, and I have only been privy to a few moments of this woman's ranting. I am jarred from my thoughts as the doorbell to the office rings. The outside doors are kept locked for security reasons. I jump up to answer, so the counselors can continue their sessions, and this kind and gentle looking man is standing in the doorway smiling at me. *No way*, I think. *You cannot be the ogre that the shouting lady is talking about. There's just no way.* As I hold the door and let him walk beside me towards the office, I check his head for horns. *Nope.*

He quietly knocks on the door, and although I cannot see her, I picture her springing off the chair to the door. As he walks, his wife continues with the list of wrongs, but the sound of her voice abruptly stops when the quiet knock is heard from behind the door.

The door swings open, and she sticks her head outside.

"You're early," she barks at him and points to the chairs, as if telling Fido to sit in his place during mealtime. As she does so, she looks up and notices I am sitting quietly. To be honest, my mother told me never to stare, but I can't help myself. To make it worse, I think my mouth is gaping open. She and I make eye contact for a split second, but I know she does not see me. And that is okay. She is too involved in her own story, so even if she had been sitting with me for the past 40 minutes, I doubt she would have seen me then either. I feel bad for her and look away, feeling sympathy because she is missing the point. I say a little prayer that she is never brought to her knees by life in the way I have been.

The husband sits quietly in the chair that she has directed him to, waiting to be called into the room. I look down at my planner and fumble around, wondering if I should try to make conversation. I look up and ask him if it has started to rain outside. The dark, foreboding clouds told me on my way into the office that it was a sure thing, so I think this is an easy question to spark conversation.

"A few drops here and there," he says, "but nothing too much yet." His voice is soft. His smile is genuine. I am confused.

The wife pops her head out of the now quiet room.

"Come on, we're ready for you now."

He gets up and walks toward the door, slowly, head down. He seems a little beaten up by life, to be honest. With my sick sense of humor, I can hear the "Funeral March" in my head. Better you than me, guy . . .

So, my little things for the day? It would have to be The Grief Lady, with her kind and understanding heart, helping us through this. Brendan likes her, and that is a gift, as I so want him to be okay through all of this.

Next would be the words, from prayers and poems, reaffirming the direction I am moving with my life. My daily quotes, my writing, and these gifts are guides to me, old scribes holding candles on the pathway as I make my way through a deep gorge in my life.

And last but not least, the screaming lady. She showed me how far I've come in my own life. I can recall a time where I was wound tight and caught in my own story. I could not see the good in the situation, and it took me a long time, a divorce, and a move to a different country to find it.

So, thank you, screaming lady. You've reminded me of a lot today. The fact that I am at a place of peace at this time in my life is a big, not a little, thing. I hope someday you can find that peace as well, and I hope it can happen without a painful journey of your own.

August 28th: You Gotta Have Faith

*Faith . . . is the art of holding on to things your reason has once accepted,
in spite of your changing moods.*

~C.S. Lewis~

It's been a hard day. I've been emotional, and I've felt the tears and
sorrow bubbling up within me since I awoke this morning. I feel
weakened and slightly frustrated by the feeling. You see, I find that
I am tiring of the roller coaster ride of emotions. I feel that
descriptor is lacking, for at least a roller coaster gives you a hint of
what's to come with the click, click sound as your car climbs the
steep incline in preparation for the terrifying drop. You have an
idea that something is about to happen. But with this, I find I am
feeling strong, and then all of a sudden, without any click or other
warning sign, I fall. Today is a day like that.

A person called me regarding an appointment this morning. And
when I answered the telephone, the first words she said breathlessly
were, "I have some really bad news."

My reaction was instinctive, and I could feel the acid beginning to
burn in the pit of my stomach. My muscles were tightening around
my bones, and I was physically bracing myself. For an instant, I
thought, "Not again God. Please, please, I cannot be hurt like this
anymore."

"I have to cancel your appointment," she said.

She was generally sorry for the inconvenience she had caused and
quickly talked about a rescheduling option. I muffled my way
through the conversation, saying yes to whatever she was saying.
As I hung up the phone, the tears shot out from my eyes, and I
sobbed loudly. My chest was beating fast, my throat was tight, and
my gut just ached. It is an intense and burning pain I feel, worse
than any injury or illness I have ever experienced.

Really bad news. It's all relative, isn't it? When I heard those words, I immediately thought of what was most important in my life, and it had nothing to do with things like appointments or life in general. It was all about love, the special people who could, even in my grief, make my heart sing.

And her words, though quickly explained, struck me in a way that completely derailed me for most of the day. Because they reminded me of something. These kinds of things happen all the time. People who have lost and hurt don't move to the back of the line, not to be hurt again until it is their cosmic turn. Things happen that we cannot understand and when we least expect them. That scares me.

I push through the day, thinking about this concept at length. I've been working through some of this fear-based thinking for weeks, to be honest. I had quite a bit to work through when Brendan started back at hockey, or when we went for a swim. One particular day at the beach, I watched Brendan and Brady take quite a spill from the sea Kayak, and I held my breath until I could see the both of them pop up from beneath the water. And then, there's the general stuff. Brendan leaving for school, Brady going out to work in the yard. And me, left to work through my doomsday mentality.

With motherhood came a deep sense of worry for me. I would worry about the potential consequences of child's play, what could happen, who could get hurt. I worried about the most inconsequential things. I would come home from a particularly tough emergency room shift and announce to Stephen he must never ride a motorcycle or a snowmobile or a horse, let alone try any substance given to him by a stranger, drink from someone else's water bottle, or run with scissors. For a while there, I was the queen of contemplation when it came to the worst-case scenario.

But then, I let some of it go. I was still super protective over my children, but I lightened up a bit. I would still tell Stephen not to walk home alone at night as he finished his junior year at college, and he would laugh with me; but I understood that he was going to be okay. Perhaps it was due to the fact I was no longer working in health care. I was not seeing those consequences each day, and it gave me a chance to exhale. Or perhaps it was my choice in partners—a husband who loved adventure and yet everything just seemed to work out. But for some reason, I had a more balanced look on the potential outcomes of situations.

And then Stephen died. I still hate using those two words together.

When that happened, I was groundless. Everything I had contemplated had, in fact, come to pass. I was right all along and wrong to let my guard down. Groundless. I've listened to some of what Pema Chödrön says about that feeling, and it comforts me to know I am not alone and that it is a normal part of being human. As a Buddhist teacher, she has offered me yet another perspective as I think about my personal spiritual journey.

It has been quite the trip. In some ways, I feel like it has been a crash course in spirituality. I was raised Roman Catholic, and our church has been a big part of our healing. But I have read and listened to other religious leaders, wanting to hear more and find out more about the differences and similarities. I'm not sure why I have been on this quest of sorts. I suppose it stems from the fact that my faith was the only thing I felt I had left when I lost Stephen.

With that being the case, I guess I am searching so I can be well informed and refine my spirituality skills. And what I've found is through all of the teachings and readings and denominations, one thing keeps coming back to me. The answer is love. It is the only answer, the only thing to fix a broken heart, a broken relationship, and a broken world. I like that. But I find I have to work very hard about loving *all* that surrounds me in life. Whether it is a challenging individual or a stress-filled situation, I find it difficult sometimes to give love to the harder elements of life. Sure, it is easy to love those who love me back. It is easy to love the butterflies, the beach, puppies, or chocolate. But what about someone you know has hurt you in the past and looks to be hurting you again? What about giving love to a situation like this one, losing your son and no longer recognizing yourself in the mirror?

This is what occupies my mind as I work through what to believe, how to act, how to go on with my life. How do I let go of the fear and embrace all the beautiful, moving parts of complete faith in something? How can I completely embrace the love?

I can't spend my life worrying about the worst-case scenario or the next horrendous phone call. Fear is not real. It is all in your head. Nor can I spend my life saying the spiritual answer is love and then in the next breath tell you who qualifies as loveable.

Because when I do attach conditions to my faith, I don't feel the connection. And I don't like not feeling connected with the power bigger than me and with Stephen's spirit.

It is hard, relinquishing what control you thought you had over your life.

So, today, I am thankful for my faith. For what it is now and what it is growing into each day.

And I am thankful for the cancelled appointment. It reminds me that I still have some work to do on letting go of the fear and anxiety. It reminds me of the simple truth. I could get another call, or another hurt or another disaster in my life. It is part of life and is not to be feared but accepted as part of your path if it should come.

I am thankful.

August 30th: Back to the Basics of a Grateful Life

The world is a looking-glass and gives back to every
man the reflection of his own face. Frown at it, and it
will in turn look sourly upon you; laugh at it and with it,
and it is a jolly, kind companion . . .

~William Makepeace Thackeray~

You know what I believe? We used to have it figured out. Before
gratitude journals, people served. People understood that they were
responsible to help out in church and school. My parents were
prime examples of that. They did not need to remind themselves to
be thankful each day by writing it in a book purchased at Barnes
and Noble or Amazon. They were thankful each day because in
their service of others in need, their own blessings were illuminated.
And in the service of others, they came to understand that the act of
helping others was the biggest act of gratitude for their own lives.

So, in my own gratitude, how can I show that dignified resilience?
How can I look outward and show my gratitude? How can I share
with others who need me, find a new way for me to channel the
love I gave to Stephen all of these years? It's a pretty big share of
love. I've got a lot to give. In fact, there's much more. As I've always
told my children, *your heart is an amazing thing. There is always room*
to love one more person.

It is all starting to come together for me.

August 31st: How Much is Postage to Heaven?

Life is God's novel. Let him write it.

~Isaac Bashevis Singer~

The letter from God really made a difference in my life. I never thought that would happen. I am thankful for that today. And it has started the wheels turning for other letters I need to write.

I have started to write letters to my family that will be here when it is my time to go. For the people who mean something to me, I want to make sure they have something that reflects my feelings after I am gone. But more importantly, I've decided I will be writing some of those messages and sending them right now. The lessons I've learned from all of this have helped me understand the importance of telling people you love them. Here and now. I have postponed those moments in life in my past, prioritizing an important presentation or housework or some other triviality. I will work in my life to not make those choices going forward.

I am thankful, because to be honest, Stephen and I really did communicate our feelings openly and often. I am blessed with that comfort, and I know that.

But I wanted to write him one more letter. Here it is.

Dear Stephen,

I miss you. Those three words do not describe my feelings of absolute anguish sufficiently. In the past weeks, I have poured words from my soul in the hopes of letting out all of this pain. Sometimes, I feel I need to invent my own words, some new ones in the dictionary that will adequately describe what it feels like to lose someone as special as you. But I know in my heart there are no words for sorrow as deep as this. I also know it needs no explanation to anyone else.

I've been thinking about writing you this letter since I heard from God. His words really helped me, and I thought it may also help to articulate my feelings to you. To tell you all of the things I've thought about since you went to heaven.

First, I love you so much. The past weeks have been a time of reflection for me, and I can see clearly the depth of the love we had. I always knew we had something incredibly special, and looking back has not only confirmed that bond, but it has also strengthened it. It is a bittersweet feeling for me, to look and realize it was as special as I thought and to know it has now changed.

When my phone rang on the evening of July 4th, I smiled as I looked at the caller ID. I thought it was you. Oh, Stephen, I feel so sad when I think about that moment. That instant, my life changed. I need you to know that I would have changed places with you if God had let me. I would have done anything to keep you safe. I do not understand God's entire plan, but I hope you can see that I've decided to put my faith in it. I know that you understand all of it now, so I hope you are looking down on me and are proud of the decisions I am making as I work through this.

I've thought about it a lot, and I know you felt my love up to the moment of your death. I want you to know that Brady and I knew how much you loved us. We felt it, and you showed it every single day. Sometimes I wish you could confirm you knew, call me up on the telephone, or come home and we could have one of our famous late-night chats. I loved those chats, where we would stay up half the night and talk about everything under the sun. I cherished those times with you, when it was quiet and just the two of us and you would tell me about your life, good and bad. I miss those times, but I know you communicate in your own way, helping me find emails and text messages and journal entries.

The thing is, I know that I did not really have anything unsaid. I know what we had and how much we loved. I wish I could shake this feeling of unfinished business. Perhaps it was the quickness of it all. Brady and I were talking and laughing about you in one minute, happy that you were with your friends and having a good time and the next, it was over. Since that time, I've racked my brain about what we last talked about and realized it was simple things, the mundane. I don't know why that bothers me so. I don't know why I feel we should have had some earth-shattering discussion. I mean, it's not like you could see this coming.

I think this is why I am writing every day, Stephen. I look at this as my last conversation with you, for a while anyway. I look at this book as one of my late-night chats with the most amazing boy.

In case I didn't tell you enough, I wanted to put down a few thoughts. In a bulleted list, of course:

You have been the greatest gift, and I feel blessed and honored that God allowed me to be your mother, even for a brief period of time. It is all so clear to me now, what your life meant to the big picture of things. You have affected so many and touched so many lives with your quiet and unassuming nature: your capacity for love and kindness, your tolerance, and your ability to know what people needed to feel safe in their lives and then give it to them. I was so proud of you when you were alive, but that pride grows since your passing, if you can believe that. I've heard so many stories about you, and they have all reaffirmed what I knew about my baby boy. I always felt you were special, the best part of myself. You made me want to be a better mother and human being, and I learned more from you than you will ever know. Thank you for being such a gift, such a precious and wonderful son.

Your brother aches for you quietly. He and I talk at bedtime, and I wish I could offer him more comfort. But there are no answers for this hurt. I remember all the private moments the two of you would have, and I know he longs for those right now. We continue to love him as hard as we can, but there is a void in his life. I feel you with him. Through his pain, he has been so strong. Please continue to watch over him and love him, to protect him and guide him.

Our life was filled with adventure, some good and some not so good. But we always made it through. As I have reflected on that journey, I've thought a lot about the last 4 years. I watched you blossom, and I could feel your happiness. Brady and I actually talked about it on our drive to the lake. Your friends told us that at the lake, you kept saying, "Isn't this the most perfect day?" Stephen, I hope it was for you. I hope your heart was filled with happiness, all that you deserved in your last moments of life. I hope we loved you hard enough, told you enough how great and awesome you were, hugged you enough, believed in you enough. I hope that it all was enough and that you felt complete and happy. I pray every day that was the case.

God told me that you were never alone, and that Matthew came to guide you home. Wow. I wish I could have seen that one. I always knew there was an unspoken longing for him throughout your life, and knowing you are together is one of the biggest things that gives me solace and peace in my heart. Was it wild to see him, to hug and to finally feel together? Promise me, when it is my time that you will both come for me. If seeing you both together is the only part of heaven I can witness, it would be enough.

I feel you when I am writing, and some of what is coming out onto the paper feels like you to be honest. I hope you can see me, and I hope you are proud of the choices I am making as I mourn. I'm not sure I understand it, but I've felt I've known what I needed to do to honor you from that moment at the lake.

Say hello to Nanny and Poppy, Matthew, Aunt Kay, Uncle Denny, Aunt Barb, Aunt Joan, and all the rest of our family. I know you are engulfed with love.

Stephen, we miss you so much. But we believe that you are doing something special in heaven. And we know your death has sparked something special here on earth. Watch over us and guide us, help us keep the faith on those dark days when we can't imagine going on without you.

I love you, my sweet baby boy.

Mom

xoxo

Today, as I prepare to enter yet another new month, check off another milestone of time passing, I am thankful. I am thankful because I know whatever I wrote in this letter, he already knew. He already knew.

September 1st: Returning to Civility

Never take a person's dignity: it is worth everything to them, and nothing to you.

~Frank Barron~

The world is a good place, you know. There is more kindness than not, no matter what the evening news tries to tell you. I've stopped watching the evening news. I decided: Why bother listening to a group of people sensationalize someone else's pain for ratings and the top-of-the-hour news flash? So, now, when I do come across something, I look innocently at my husband and say, "When did that happen?" It has been a freeing and uplifting experience for me. I made the decision to do so when I saw how they distorted the life of my son in a few simple words. In the stories immediately following his death, they painted a picture of a boy from the snippets of information they could get. They had not had an opportunity to speak with anyone who loved him and knew him. So, instead of a story that should have read, "A beautiful, talented, loving boy died today. He was a rising senior at NC State, a goalie, a brother, a son, a good person. He was an amazing human being that could have given so much to the world, and now he is gone . . ."

Instead, it read like this . . .

"Alcohol was found at the scene, but no one could confirm if this was a factor in the accident."

In one sentence, the media had painted a picture of my child that had nothing to do with his time on earth. It truly was irrelevant. I know I have written about this before. But it really bothered me. As my friend Tracey said, they did not say "there were hot dogs and chips at the scene, but no one could confirm if he ate any and if that contributed to his death." So, combine that sensationalized reporting with the anonymous hate speak on the news site discussion boards, and you've got yourself a whole big ball of negativity swirling around a family whose world has just imploded.

I read one discussion board where one guy questioned the tryouts and athleticism requirements for university sports, because obviously, Stephen was not a great athlete if he could not even make it across the cove.

I don't know why I could not let it go. But it has started a personal crusade for me. I am only one voice, but I vow to speak out about this from now until the day I die. Give hurting families the dignity they deserve. We've created this world where everyone feels entitled to comment on someone else's misfortune. We've created a world where it is expected that you will be judged if you are put in the public eye. In fact, if you read a news story online, it is the last thing they ask of you. *Click here to comment on this story.* They encourage it. Why are we having a challenging time finding good leaders in this world? Why do you hear people say you would have to be "nuts to get into politics"?

The answer is simple. People see what happens to others in the public eye. And they quietly look at themselves and see they have imperfections too. They may be a great leader, but they did have that DUI in college. Our judgments are not only preventing us from evolving as individuals. We are, by virtue of our own need to feel empowered, preventing our world from being the best it can be. It's a big statement, I know, but think about it. And all of this came to me by watching how people treated the death of my son. Even in the death of a truly innocent and beautiful human being, people found a way to talk about the dark side of life, assuming there had to be a negative backstory.

So, I am thankful for my media diet. I love succeeding with a diet. I am thankful for my voice and my courage to say something about this, even if my family and close friends are the only ones who listen. And finally, I am thankful for sharing my first 20 pages of writing with Brady. Big step! He takes the papers from me as if they are treasures. I do love him so. Because I know that even if he begins to read and sees I have typed the same word over and over for 20 pages, he would still love me. Let's hope he finds it a little more interesting than that. Thank you.

September 2nd: My 12-Year-Old Teacher and Rudy the Wonder Dog

You think dogs will not be in heaven? I tell you, they will be there long before any of us.

~Robert Louis Stevenson~

Brendan has been a talker since birth. I mean it, even in the first months of his time on earth, the baby babble was loud and purposeful, and there was lots of it. It seems he has always had something to say. He started to talk early, and from that moment, his speech was clear and funny and dramatic.

In kindergarten, during our interview with his teacher, she informed us that she and Brendan would, at some point, every day have a one-on-one conversation at her desk, usually when the other kids were having play time. She said it was almost as if he needed some more adult conversation. He has always been verbally advanced and has had an ability to describe his feelings or events with clarity and detail beyond his years.

That talent has not changed as he has grown but in fact has sharpened. Along with his attention to detail, he has now developed a sharp sense of humor with a touch of sarcasm, which may or may not be hereditary.

In any case, Brendan's conversations are a source of gratitude for me. To see life through his eyes is such a pleasure, such an escape. He talks more than Stephen did, although I still believe he is just as introspective.

So, today I am thankful for the hour after Brendan gets home from school. For today, Brendan spoke for 17 minutes straight, with barely a breath in between. He had so much to say, about school and friends and about hockey.

On and on he went—there was simply so much to tell me. And I was touched by his enthusiasm for life. I was humbled, yet again, by the courage of another. You see, I watched my son, who had suffered as much loss as I did this summer, and he was talking about all the good in his life. He could barely catch a breath as he tried to get it all out.

The wonder of a child will teach us. I believe that. I believe that we grown-ups lose something when we decide to leave the trivial and the simple joys behind for more grown-up things. We exchange play clothes for business suits and begin to layer things on top of our lives that dull our senses—not only our senses of joy and happiness but also the joy found within loss, the joy of resilience.

So, today, I have gratitude for my teacher Brendan. He is a model for how we should all conduct ourselves in pain.

I am also thankful for my other teacher, Rudy the Wonder Dog. I know that sounds like my higher education has gone to the dogs . . . insert groan here for the bad joke. But Rudy has been a constant source of comfort and a valued teacher through all of this. That morning, almost two months ago now, Rudy stood by me in one of the most difficult moments of my life. He did so with a quiet, unconditional love. I can recall one moment that morning at the lake, where I cried out in despair. And he looked up at me with eyes as deep as the ocean and licked my hand. We stared at each other for a long time, having an unspoken conversation of comfort. If we are all lucky enough to have either a person or animal show us the meaning of unconditional love, we have already reached a heaven of sorts. I am blessed because I have a houseful of people who love one another without expectation.

Rudy is not an alpha dog. He does not run around trying to exert power. Any child could jump on his back, and he would play with them, but he would never force them away or hurt them. He simply surrenders to his reality. And because he is easy with the world and with his life, life returns the favor. He does not have the struggles of other dogs that fight for control or power in their house. Because he does not exert his strength, he has been anointed as a Wonder Dog. He acts almost human, lying on the couch as if he used his Visa to pay for it. He is at complete peace with his circumstances.

I have learned much from this chocolate lab, who, as I type, is lying at my feet. I have learned that a life of struggle is only a reality if you choose to make it a struggle. I have learned about surrendering to the *now* of my life. And I have learned that the truly rich in this world are those who can love unconditionally.

September 3rd: Technical Difficulties, Pictures, and Insights on Parenting

He who teaches children learns more than they do.

~German Proverb~

Have you ever had a moment in your life where you feel so frustrated that you feel your head may actually just pop off and fly through the air, never to be seen again, the decapitation releasing the steam within you from whatever irritant has caused you to completely lose your cool?

Well, there is one thing that can do that to me. Computer issues— technical difficulties or anything related to a problem with household technology. I can usually keep my cool and sense of humor in the worst of situations. I have learned that lately. But give me a corrupted file, a faulty cord, or the "blue screen of death," and I melt down like a badly built nuclear plant.

It is one of many flaws, but it is very noticeable. I really feel for my husband, as he is usually on the receiving end of some of the lava spewing from my mouth when I cannot get the computer to do as I wish. You see, the computer does not talk back, and I need some validation. Poor guy.

Today was one of those days, where technology and I face off, like the McCoy's and the Hatfields. And as much as I have never been a person to give up, I have to admit to you that I never win. I modify, I accept. I go through the five stages of grief over my loss of control. I'm not sure if Elizabeth Kübler-Ross envisioned her theory applied in this area of life.

I am trying to access a document. It is important, and I need it today. I have saved it in an obscure location, and the computer does not want to share it with me. Try after try, I search, but it is not working.

I smile as I remember the look of horror on Stephen's face when he would look over my shoulder as I was working and exclaim, "Mom, you cannot have that many windows open at the same time! You need to close some!" Okay, well, I need to be honest. I never took his advice on all things computer, and I am now paying the price.

And then, the most amazing thing happens. Because as I am simmering in my desk chair, I open an electronic folder that turns out to be the best gift of my day—my week, for that matter. My mind shifts from my frustration and my old responses and back into gratitude.

Inside this unlabeled folder sits pictures, the most fantastic records of happy times. For a moment, I hold my breath. I had long since forgotten about those pictures—and because of it, the details of those occasions.

It was funny, because it was as if I had created this folder to assemble a timeline of sorts, as the pictures were from all of the stages of my life with Stephen. The little boy, so cute and pleasant, with an endless amount of energy. The 11-year-old, baseball uniform, with a catcher's glove on and pure ambition on his face. He always wanted to win. The teenager, the smile a little more guarded, but still there. So many stories, so many journeys in these few precious photos. The teenage smile, holding back from the usual angst of adolescence but also from hurt. And then the shift. I still can't figure out why I clumped these all together. But sitting next to that smile is a picture of Stephen at the beach with Brady. July 4, 2008, exactly one year before his death. They are playing bocce ball, and as usual, they are laughing about some random piece of information. I had been sitting under the gazebo, sheltered from the hot July sun, just watching them. Content. That would be the word I would use to describe the mood of the day. Surrounded by friends and family, just the way I like it. I had clicked away with my camera. And I had captured this sequence of pictures that are now like precious gems to us. There is a look on Stephen's face as he laughs with Brady, and well, it just says all that needs to be said. If God were able to articulate what he wanted for each of us during our time on earth, it would be a moment like this one. Not the houses, the cars, the perfect children, or the two vacations a year. No, I believe God would tell us that we would be fulfilled if we could learn how to accept the simple moments of joy. And I am thankful, because my son, with the love of my husband, had so much joy on that day.

Taking photographs is something I am very thankful for. It is fantastic to capture those memories, to click at just the right moment. I loved it before, and now, well, I am just so blessed to have taken so many pictures.

This folder read like a good novel and told a story. As I studied each photo, I could see Stephen grow in size and in maturity. But the most striking thing I noticed was the "growth of happiness." You can see the light within him grow as if someone had thrown kerosene on the fire that burned within him.

I am thankful. I am thankful for that light and for how brightly it was shining at the time of his death. Oh, if only I can be so lucky. If only we can all be so lucky to shine brightly from within at any point in our lifetimes.

And I guess by the sheer connection of it all, I have to say I am thankful for the technical difficulties. Without them, I would not have found this hidden treasure.

September 5th: There's Never a Moment Like the Moment

It isn't what you have or who you are or where you are or what you are
doing that makes you happy or unhappy. It is what you think about it.
~Dale Carnegie~

I've decided to turn all this writing into something more than a
word document. I'm going to publish this, my record of events, my
memoir of grief and gratitude. I don't know who will read it. But I
feel I need to share my journey in the hopes that someone else may
read it and be reassured in knowing the sun will indeed rise
tomorrow.

I feel compelled. It's like I've been let in on some magic secret and I
can't keep my mouth shut. I feel so absolutely broken and fixed, all
at the same time. I have this feeling that I have somehow found my
purpose, having only discovered it by losing everything else.

I do this for Stephen. He deserves to have a book written about him.
His life is worthy of celebrating and honoring and learning from.
He has been the most influential human being in my life, and it is a
story worth telling. Boy, do I miss him. And those five words are
inadequate in the description of the ache that sits within my heart as
I contemplate the next two months without him and the next two
after that and so on.

I need to share in the hopes that my simple words can spark a
conversation about life and faith. Maybe it is because I want to talk
about how we communicate how we feel to the people that matter. I
keep telling myself that Stephen knew. I told him often, and I
believe he knew. But what about other people in my life?

Today, I am thankful for a word document that keeps me going, a boy that changed my life, and Kleenex.

September 6th: Patience is a Virtue, Kelly Dear

How poor are they that have not patience!

What wound did ever heal but by degrees?

~William Shakespeare~

I find myself sometimes becoming very frustrated that I am still, at certain points in the week, a basket case, according to my estimation. I think the frustration stems from the fact that at other points, I feel like I am somewhat strong, and I am doing it. And then a song, a scent, a picture, a memory will hit me like a brick, and I will be reduced to tears and sobs for Stephen. It is a strange sensation, "the hit," as I call it. It is both emotional and physical. My mind and heart dealing with the emotion of the situation and my body dealing with the physical sensation of a blow to the chest with a sledgehammer.

It bothers me, as I have always felt I was in control of my emotions. I took pride in my ability to put on the stoic "strong woman" face in the midst of the most stressful times of my life. No one knew of my pain—or at least that is what I thought. But with my grief for Stephen, I am not driving the bus. I don't feel in control of my pain, and I feel forced to go with the flow. I want to get to a place where the pain is not as intense, where my shoulders are not weighed down with the sadness, as if I were wearing lead shoulder pads.

But as my mother and so many before her always said, "Patience is a virtue." I must be patient and not rush this journey. I want to come out on the other side with the wisdom I need to continue to live a life of happiness. Someday.

So, today, I will be grateful for patience. I am not always good at it, but I keep trying. And knowing that my grief is a measure of my love for Stephen, I really don't want to rush it.

Patience is also a form of action.

~Auguste Rodin~

September 18th: It Will Never Be the Same

Courage doesn't always roar. Sometimes courage is the little voice at the end of the day that says I'll try again tomorrow.

~Mary Anne Radmacher~

Same house, same husband, same son, same bills, same responsibilities. But it is nothing like it was before.

Things have changed. Forever.

A well-meaning person had actually pointed this out to me, blurting out, "My gosh, this is so awful; nothing will ever be the same. I don't know how you will go on."

At first, I took offense. But leaving out the "not going on" part, she was right.

The challenge I face in grief is the perspective. It hurts—there is no changing that. But how I will persevere and thrive depends on what viewpoint I decide to take with my grief. I can either see life as ugly and not worth living or I can see it as imperfect but beautiful.

I have decided to embrace my new reality, even though it feels like embracing a bush of thorns.

This journey has been an awakening for me. The important things have been illuminated, and I can see what truly matters. It's not the material things or the trivial that we busy our life with each and every day. Life is not what we do or what we have, it is how we love.

And despite the devastating loss, I am thankful for the vision of the truth I have received from it. I still cry often. I miss my sweet boy. But I believe I will be a better person for walking through this valley. I believe I can become that person by sharing my insight, no matter how hard it was to receive the lesson. I have to believe that, because I cannot entertain the alternative.

Some days, I wonder if I'm going to make it. Some days, I struggle to find my one good thing. But I keep trying and start each day anew. No matter how I got here, I am thankful for my new reality.

October 29th: Sunny Days

Keep your face always toward the sunshine — and the shadows will fall behind you.

~Walt Whitman~

Sunny days. I never thought I would return to a place of appreciation for the blue skies and bright sunshine of the Carolinas. But as I sit gazing out my office window this morning, I am welcoming the warmth of the morning sun as it dances on the walls. I can't remember when I started to notice it again. There was a time I wondered if it would be, as it was on the inside, perpetually cloudy. I still do wonder if that is not my fate, but I keep working to find the good. So, I must celebrate the sun today.

The sunshine is back. It is just as beautiful, but I also appreciate it more. I see the value of a sunny day after ones of clouds, rain, and gloom. This does not mean I will not be in tears at some point today, but I am taking the sunshine as it comes. For now, I need my shades. I am thankful that I remember that the sun is always behind the clouds.

November 12th: The Magic of Hockey Players

It is foolish and wrong to mourn the men who died. Rather we should thank God that such men lived.

~George S. Patton~

The team retired Stephen's jersey today. They've done so much to show their love and support. Today was a really hard day.

We arrived at the rink to see a packed house. I was surrounded by my family, and my best friend was by my side. Immediately upon entering the arena, I began to physically hurt. It was as if every muscle in my body had decided to cramp up, weary from the constant exertion as I attempted to hold myself together. My entire body was tensed so that I could hold back a complete collapse. I wondered if anyone noticed.

The last time I had been here was to watch my boy play. I remember standing just inside the doors of the arena, watching Stephen mentally prepare himself for the game. He had always stood outside the locker room alone, collecting his thoughts and putting on his game face. I knew not to go up and start a conversation; this was part of his goalie ritual. Instead, I would wait patiently for my hug and kiss that would come after three periods of hockey had been played. For that moment, I would look at him from a distance, watching him get ready to stand on his head. Then, just as he was just about to step onto the ice, we would make eye contact for a moment, and I would smile. No words were necessary.

Watching Stephen play hockey was like watching a compressed version of life. Strength, courage, overcoming adversity, humility — you could see all of it in three periods of hockey. I will be honest, I never found it easy to watch. Most times, I both held my breath and said a Hail Mary all at the same time. I couldn't stand with anyone else, my husband included. I had to stand and pace and bang on the plexiglass when he made an amazing save. I had to distance myself from the other fans, because at times, I swore like a sailor. It was so thrilling to watch him play.

But not tonight. Tonight, we were here to remember and honor him. The tickets say so. Oh, the pain in my chest. Oh, the absolute ache in my throat. I must keep it in.

As we awaited the start of the ceremony, we greeted old friends. I could feel the eyes of some on us, as they realized we were the parents. We were the family of the dead boy, here to have him honored for who he was.

My God. Please let me hold this all in.

The ceremony was so touching. The lights dimmed; they had Stephen's jersey hanging in the net with a spotlight shining on it. It just broke my heart all over again. As we waited to be called out to accept the jersey, and for the unveiling of the banner, I tried to compose myself. But every damn time I looked at the jersey, I felt like I could die at any moment. All I could see was the image of him just months before alive, vibrant, determined, and competitive. And now, a lonely jersey swung on a pole.

Brady spoke, and even Brendan was brave enough to say a few words, telling his team to beat the Tar Heels. My brave boy. He is so much stronger than me. And I thought I was going to make it, until the music started and each of Stephen's teammates, as they prepared to leave the ice, skated past the goal, touched the jersey, and tapped the posts.

It was his final sendoff. And my heart broke all over again.

I was so grateful for the way they had honored him. I was humbled. I was at a loss for words and so, so thankful for the way they had honored him. I only wish that every mother could be as lucky as I was that night, to bear witness to the impact your child has made on the people who knew him.

I may be biased, but I think there is something special about hockey players. They are creatures of tradition and habit, history and honor. They have a deep respect for the game and for each other, both on and off the ice. They show up to the arena in suits and ties. They don smelly equipment and skate on blades of steel, crushing each other into the boards, fighting like mad dogs over a black disc. Two of them will stand in front of this frozen black disc, in the hopes they get hit by it. But what happens on that ice is magic because it turned my boy into a man. It turned his teammates into the type of men that took the time to remember him in this incredibly special way.

I am thankful.

November 25th: Gobble Gobble

To speak gratitude is courteous and pleasant, to enact gratitude is generous and noble, but to live gratitude is to touch Heaven.

~Johannes A. Gaertner~

What a difference a year makes. I am thinking about the Thanksgiving table and preparations today. What it looks like today versus what it looked like last year. There is a dramatic difference.

Last year, the table was one of anticipation. With plates and arrangements and serving dishes, the table sat in wait of the coming day. The house was busy with the workings of the holiday. Smells drifted from the kitchen throughout the house. Spices that are used once yearly combined to create an aroma that only Thanksgiving can produce.

Most importantly, there was so much movement in the house. Thumps and bumps could be heard all over the house as two brothers played upstairs. One, excited to see his big brother again, home from university. The other, a grown man in his own right, happy to be home in this safe haven, where he could regress back to being a kid and have his parents take care of him again, even if only for three or four days. Last year, our beautiful son brought home a friend with him, and we enjoyed the company of another and delighted in the knowing that our son was surrounding himself with such good people.

We sat around the table last year, held hands, and said what we were thankful for. In our descriptions, each one of us talked about the simple things: the food, the company, and the smiles. It is a beautiful memory but one that is bittersweet as we approach Thanksgiving, the first one without Stephen. I think back to that moment, to those people, living and laughing, not knowing that in one short year, all would be changed.

This year, our house is different. On our dining room table, there are no serving dishes sitting in anticipation. Instead, a framed hockey jersey sits on the table, given to us by his teammates after the team retired his number. There are no leaves from the garden, flickering candles, napkin holders. Just the jersey, sitting on the table, reminding us. The aromas are here but limited. We are going to spend Thanksgiving with friends this year, as the thought of sitting around the table without the chairs filled to capacity is simply too much to bear.

The quiet of the house is deafening. We are all sticking pretty close together this year. We feel the difference, but there are no words to describe it. It is, as the three of us look at one another, as if no words are necessary. We all just feel it: the ache, the longing for him.

So, on this first Thanksgiving without him, what can I be thankful for?

I can be grateful for memories. I have some really good ones. And I pray each night that they will sustain me through this holiday season. I am thankful for my husband and son, who stick close, as we together face the hardest of days. We are sad, but we are together. I am thankful for friends and family, who envelope us with love, and "Handle us with Care" as we journey through this year of *Firsts*.

And finally, I am thankful for the privilege of having been a mother to the most amazing boy. Before Stephen's death, I often wondered how I was so lucky to have him as a son. Am I sad? Yes, at moments it is overwhelming, and my sadness is as deep as the ocean. But I am also grateful.

This year, when I bow my head in thanks, my gratitude will not be the usual standard responses. I will be thankful through tears. This year, I am going to take my time and savor that moment, because it is the moments of thankfulness that are truly saving us.

December 3rd: Jolly Ranchers and the Automotive Aisle

*Some people succeed in spite of hardships. Others succeed because of them.
The truth is our problems help to make us what we are. Those who suffer
often learn the value of compassion. Those who struggle often learn
perseverance. And those who fall down often teach others how to rise
again. Our troubles can shape us in ways a carefree existence cannot.*

~Steve Goodier~

It's not really easy for me to go out. I have difficulty admitting that,
even to myself. I used to be this strong woman. But now, I'm just
raw. I'm just so very broken. When I go out, I find it difficult to talk.
I am particularly sensitive to negativity. I am distracted. On a recent
trip to the grocery store, I browsed and shopped, and as I was
wheeling my cart towards my vehicle, I realized I had left it running
in the parking lot.

I am pissing myself off. I hate being this way.

But life continues, and I have to go out. I have to shop for
Christmas. So, I get ready for the day and drive to Target. I have my
list. *In and out Kelly, that's what this is going to be.* But I am already
exhausted. I feel like I am pulling a bag of rocks around with me
wherever I go.

Inside the store, with my list in hand, I wander around the store,
pushing the cart up and down the aisles but putting nothing inside.
I've been wandering around the store for 30 minutes, and I've
checked not one item off my list.

I make my way towards the candy aisle. I'll start with something
easy, picking up treats for the kids on the list. I spot Jolly Ranchers.
Stephen loved Jolly Ranchers.

Cue waterworks now.

I can't hold it back. And of course, I have no tissues and no sunglasses. Just me and my sleeve in the candy aisle of Target. I quickly make my way to the automotive aisle, knowing I will find more solitude than in the Christmas candy section. I find a buffing cloth for car cleaning and wipe my eyes. I put it back on the shelf.

Who said it was okay to have Christmas without him? Who said it was okay to play Christmas music?

So, what am I thankful for today? Automotive wash clothes and deserted aisles in Target affording me some privacy. I am thankful that tomorrow is another day.

Oh, Stephen, I miss you so.

December 10th: I'll Have a Blue Christmas

God gave us memory so that we might have roses in December.

~James M. Barrie~

I am preparing to open up the boxes of Christmas decorations. Each box contains memories of Stephen and of happier Christmases of years gone by. I can't sugarcoat this, it is painful. It hurts, and I feel anxious about pulling back the tissue paper and seeing the ornaments we painted together when he was 11 or his First Christmas ornament. I don't know if I can handle it or if I am ready for the assault on my emotions.

As I child, one of my fondest Christmas moments would be when my father would bring in the tree and set it in the stand. It was such an exciting time, with the boxes of decorations scattered all over the living room floor, waiting to be opened and explored. He would stabilize the tree and, with his Black and Decker drill, create holes in the trunk of our Charlie Brown Christmas tree to insert more branches from a second tree he had cut down. My father would essentially make one tree from two. Before he started with the lights, he would always have to put on some occasion-appropriate music. One of the albums he loved to play was Elvis Presley's *Blue Christmas*. I can clearly recall trying to imitate the drawl of a southern boy in my Newfoundland accent. It never really worked, but I had fun just the same. Once my father finished putting on the lights, I would finally be allowed to open the boxes of ornaments. It was such a special part of our holiday. Open the box, remove the tissue paper carefully, and unroll the ornament. Looking back, I think I enjoyed this more than Christmas morning because beneath every piece of tissue paper was a memory. Our ornaments were not fancy; many were homemade. But each one told a story of a Christmas past, some funny and some sad. My parents would tell me about the different tales with each unwrapped treasure, so it is no surprise it took us most of the evening to decorate the tree.

As I reflect on my happy memories of my parents, I understand that with time, I will be able to reflect on memories of Stephen without the pain. Someday, I will be able to open boxes and look at pictures, and I will not have this same ache that now sits in my chest. But for this year, I need to just accept the ache and, when I can, let it out. Like this morning, over coffee and the morning paper, I cried and howled like an Irish banshee. I may not have learned anything about current events, but I feel so much better after letting it out.

I am thankful for my tears, as they wash away some of the pain. I am thankful that I still feel Stephen's love all around us. Love does not die.

As Elvis said, I'll have a Blue Christmas. Yep, I can't deny it. But will we survive and make it something meaningful? Yes, we will.

I am so thankful, as I have boxes and boxes of happy Christmas memories. Someday, I will be able to look at them.

December 18th: Giving a Measure of Love to Others in Stephen's Name

For each new morning with its light,

For rest and shelter of the night,

For health and food, for love and friends,

For everything Thy goodness sends.

~Ralph Waldo Emerson~

Today is a good day, and I have lots to be thankful for.

Brendan starts Christmas vacation today, and he is counting the hours until the afternoon dismissal bell releases him from the clutches of education.

As I waited to see him, I delivered presents this morning. As part of living a life of gratitude, we decided to adopt some individuals who were having a tough time and needed some help this year. My husband, son, and I talked about it and thought it would be a great thing to do this year in memory of a boy who was giving and loving every day of the year. We bought presents and wrapped them with care. One of the presents I selected for each of the families was a gratitude journal. I have come to realize that gratitude can carry you over some of the toughest parts of your life. It can't make hurt go away, but it can smooth out the rough edges. I figured I would pass the lesson of gratitude along, with a wish that it helps them through as well.

It feels good to let this love out. I have all this love for Stephen bursting at the seams, and maybe I can give a measure of it to someone else who needs it this year.

I am thankful. Maybe someone who needs it will feel love this Christmas because of him.

December 24th: The True Gifts of Christmas

Christmas gift suggestions: To your enemy, forgiveness. To an opponent, tolerance. To a friend, your heart. To a customer, service. To all, charity. To every child, a good example. To yourself, respect.

~Oren Arnold~

Well, the gifts are wrapped and sitting under the tree. The music plays softly in the background, and familiar smells float from the kitchen. The lights are sparkling, and it is simply beautiful. As I look around, I feel blessed for what surrounds me in my life, the biggest of all the treasures being love. I have so much love around me. But inside my chest, there is an ache that will not go away. As I look to the mantle, Stephen's stocking is hung with care, put there by his little brother. He had talked to me about it, and we thought it would be nice to hang it. I have a feeling that Santa may bring some special treats for charities that need them tonight. On the branches of our tree, the ornaments sit as reminders of his time with us. Funny, happy memories.

Last Christmas, the house was filled with a flurry of activity, and we could hear the laughter coming from Brendan's bedroom as he and Stephen played games and wrapped presents. I can remember the excited looks of anticipation as they handed me the presents to open on Christmas morning. Little did I know that we were making treasured memories, ones that we now hold onto for dear life as Christmas Eve is once again upon us.

So, what in the heck could I possibly be thankful for on this first Christmas Eve without my precious Stephen?

I am thankful for the family that remains and for how hard we are working to be happy. We don't always succeed, and sometimes we cry. No—correct that—we cry a lot. But we recover, and we are determined to enjoy the special moments of the season. We are resilient, and I am proud of that fact.

I am thankful for my faith and how I have a new respect and understanding for the "Reason for the Season."

I am thankful for the wisdom that the past 5 and a half months have given me. Even with the ache, I am drinking up every moment of this day and the days to come. I understand that we are making memories, and we only get one chance at making the good ones. So, even though the memories will be tinged with sadness and longing for Stephen, I know that I will look back on them years from now and feel good. I will feel proud of how we handled ourselves, of how we grieved and celebrated at the same time.

I am grateful for the family and friends and strangers who surround us with love and support and just want us to be okay. Calls and emails have shown up throughout the day, showing us that we are never far from love. People like the funeral home director in Pittsboro, North Carolina. He and his wife sent us a Christmas poinsettia to simply let us know that they were thinking of us. Imagine that. As I explained to Brendan, this man and his wife were strangers who had showed us a kindness like no other on the worst day of our lives. And, months later, they remembered us. These moments of kindness have arrived in our lives just when we needed them most. And they prove to us that there is and always will be more good in this world than bad.

And finally, as the stars sparkle in the Christmas Eve sky, I am thankful for Stephen. Of all the Christmas mornings I have experienced and will experience in years to come, he was my best gift. He showed me that the best gifts can come in small packages, and surprises are good. I wish we had more time. But knowing that could not be so, I am thankful that he was not only my son but also my teacher. I am a better human being for having the privilege to parent him.

As we await the toll of the Christmas bell to announce our Savior's birth, my heart aches for Stephen. But we still have much to be thankful for in our lives. I realize that the true gifts in life are not those who sit beneath the branches of our Christmas trees. The true gifts are the people who will open them in the morning, with smiles and grins and hugs and kisses.

December 31st: Ringing in a New Year

And ye, who have met with Adversity's blast,

And been bow'd to the earth by its fury;

To whom the Twelve Months, that have recently pass'd

Were as harsh as a prejudiced jury—

Still, fill to the Future! and join in our chime,

The regrets of remembrance to cozen.

And having obtained a New Trial of Time,

Shout in hopes of a kindlier dozen.

~Thomas Hood~

New Year's Eve: the night where we throw away the old and embrace the new. We sing the verse of "Auld Lang Syne":

". . . should old acquaintance be forgot . . ."

We never really think about the meaning of the words. New Year's Eve is a time of renewal and resolution, a time of promise for the upcoming 12 months. But it can also be a time of melancholy, of remembrance. Some will exclaim that they are glad to be waving goodbye to such a year, and others will sadly and quietly reflect on the end of the last year they had with someone so precious.

For me, I have to admit, it is a bit of both. 2009 was, by far, the toughest year I have ever experienced. I have never felt so much pain or sadness. A part of my very being was ripped away far too soon; this year will leave a permanent mark on my soul. But surprisingly enough, I can still reflect and find many blessings from the year. Simple things, like family and friends. Love shown to us in our time of need. With everything in my life stripped away, I now understand it is the simple blessings that are the real gifts of life: love, kindness, and friendship. Those are the treasures we should be searching for in this life, not flat screen TVs or name-brand anything.

So, tonight, I am reflective—on the things I've learned, and the blessings bestowed upon me and my family, even as we hurt. And as for the resolutions? Just one, and it is not even a resolution but rather an affirmation:

I will be thankful every single day.

I made a choice when I received "the call." I decided to look for little things, the goodness in life that would help me get through this unbearable pain. Some days it was easy to find the blessings, and others, I really struggled. But I did it, and it saved me and continues to save me. And in the process, I show my 12-year-old son about the power of love, faith, and resilience, even in the darkest of days. So, as 2009 comes to a close, I will light a candle and say thank you for a life that changed me forever. And I will promise to continue to live a life of gratitude, no matter what the circumstance, in 2010. And because I will live a life of gratitude, happiness will be sure to follow me wherever I go.

I think about Stephen on this last day of 2009. I can almost hear him, urging me on, exclaiming form the mountaintop:

Be happy, Mom!!

I can think of no better way to honor him.

January 8th: Bedtime Stories

Each day of our lives we make deposits in the memory banks of our children.

~Charles R. Swindoll~

I have the most wonderful quiet moments with Brendan at bedtime. He is an old soul, much like his brother was, and he is sensitive and mature well beyond his years. But how could he not be considering all that he has endured in his short life?

I have to remind myself of that sometimes, as he has seen so much more than I ever had when I was 12. Each and every day, Brady and I talk about how we can best help him navigate through the loss of his most awesome big brother, as we figure out how to get through it ourselves. Some days, I feel we have championed the cause with success. And others, I feel hopelessly and utterly inadequate in our attempts to provide comfort and answers. Because there are no answers that would really give us peace about the sudden loss of Stephen.

Last night, we had one of the good nights. We are all more emotional at the end of the day. The fatigue of life wears me down, and the sadness creeps in, and I no longer have the resilient and sunny disposition of the morning. For Brendan, he is a little quieter, and I can always sense when it is a suitable time for a bedtime chat. Last night was one of those evenings.

We lie in the dark, looking out the window, wishing and praying for the snow forecast to be true. We already have the snow day planned out, and we both pray sincerely to God that it would be a good thing for the city to be shut down. You can't blame us. We are two Canadians living in the South, and as much as we love it here, we sometimes do miss the white stuff.

The conversation is light, and I tell funny stories about him as a toddler and Stephen as the protective big brother. We giggle, and Brendan asks for one more story, to both drink up the memories and delay bedtime for another few minutes. We talk about Stephen watching over us. As we talk quietly, I realize that we are holding hands, and our hearts are open.

And it strikes me. We are giggling and smiling about the memories. At points, I can see the sadness on his face, and vice versa, but the majority of the conversation is without pain. I am thankful for that. We are moving to a point where we can recall the happy times with Stephen without complete emotional collapse.

I am thankful that we have continued to talk to Brendan and show him that expressing our emotions is a natural part of our process of grief. I am so proud of him because he feels comfortable with the discomfort. He understands it is normal, and nothing to fear, and because of it, we are working towards moments like tonight where we can remember without the anguish. I am thankful that I am giving my son happy thoughts to float around in his dreams, even if it is not always easy.

January 11th: The Evolving Meaning of Life

When compiling his great dictionary, the young Noah Webster travels to the Himalayas, where he climbs to the cave of the world's wisest man. "O, great sage," he says, "tell me the meaning of life." The sage sits Noah at his feet and, with great solemnity, commences to unfold the meaning of life. When finished, he places a hand on the young man's shoulder and says, "Do you have any other questions, my son?" Noah flips a page in his notebook and says, "You wouldn't know the meaning of lift, would you?"

~Robert Breault~

I am wondering, in my quest for gratitude, who is coming into our house and wearing our clothes and using our towels. Of all the simple things in life I can find to feel gratitude for, laundry is not one of them. And to top it off, I am the mother of a hockey player. This means I am the woman who dons a HAZMAT suit to unpack wet and dirty socks that could walk out of the bag without my assistance, socks that emit an odor that is like no other. After a particularly long weekend of playing hockey, a voice can be heard when we open this bag. It is the socks, asking:

"How you doing?"

In any case, this morning, as the washer's rhythmic tones fill our quiet house and remind me of the order of things, I am thinking about the meaning of life. Imagine living with someone like me, who connects the meaning of life with the sound of a washing machine? My husband is a saint.

Life is beautiful and delicious, and at the same time, it can be ugly and painful. It is complicated, and I marvel at how my perspective on life has changed from my teenage years to now.

As a teenager, I just knew I had it all figured out. Not only did I have it figured out, but I also believed I was advanced in my thinking. In explaining things to my parents or older siblings, I had this finality in my statements that made it seem like I had researched and knew what I was talking about. I was obviously seeing this much clearer than the rest of you, right? Wrong.

By the time I had finished nursing school, I realized that there were some things that *maybe* I did not have completely buttoned up, but I could smile, and I was sure everyone would think I did. I realized that life could sometimes present you with situations that simply gutted you, but you could put on a strong face and keep moving and everything would be okay. I blocked them, did not speak about what I did not want to deal with. It just made it easier if I kept those hurtful things in a separate compartment. Right? Wrong.

Years passed, and I realized I was not as invincible as I once thought. Nor was I as smart. I realized that life not only meant being gutted sometimes, but it also meant that you could be kicked and spit on when you were down. It could mean that everything you thought you could count on . . . you could not. Ten years ago, I started to make sense of what my parents were saying, and as I came to certain conclusions, I would inwardly cringe and wonder why I was such a slow learner. But I pressed on with a self-assured outer image, giving the impression I knew the right path and direction, all the while desperately looking for someone with a damn map.

And now another 10 years have passed. And what do I realize?

I wasn't really wrong back then; I was just learning. And the best learning comes from hurt and mistakes. Wisdom comes when you get stomped on. It gives you perspective so you can avoid it the next time, or at least figure out how to bounce back. Wisdom comes from being in the place I am in now, knowing that it is okay to not have things all figured out.

I've learned that life is complicated, bad things happen all the time, and no one is spared. I've learned that when something bad happens to you, that doesn't mean you will go to the back of the line to be spared further until your turn comes around. I've learned not to be afraid of it but rather become still and quiet and just accept it. Fighting it changes nothing and only intensifies your pain. I have my moments of hurt and anger and protest, of course. But these days, I understand and have the tools that will allow them to pass quickly.

I've realized that the measure of life is not in years, position, letters behind your name, weight, height, ethnicity, place of birth, religion, or bank balance. I've realized the measure of a life is dependent on how far you will go each day to become a better person, how many people you treat with kindness, and how much closer you get to learning how to forgive both yourself and others.

I've learned that faith in God is personal, much like a deep and lasting friendship with someone who has seen the good, the bad, and the ugly. I've learned that true prayer is not only getting on your knees when life slaps you up the side of the head. Why do we look up when things go bad and say, "God, please make this better, please fix what is going wrong," but when things are sailing along and we are on top of the world, we look in the mirror? We somehow think it is because of what we ourselves did, and God is not in the credits. True prayer is your daily conversation with your friend, understanding that where you are is because you are together.

I've realized that faith is not about the church you attend or how loud you exclaim your beliefs or the fact that you are a Christian. It's all about the love and your own personal relationship with the Big Guy. I call him the Big Guy, as I think He likes to bring some levity into the discussion instead of having faith be all about pomp and circumstance and fear. I think it makes Him more approachable, don't you?

I've learned that the human spirit is unstoppable, and resilience is within each of us, including within 12-year-old boys.

And finally, I've learned it is all about the love. The more I surround myself with the good stuff, the closer I feel Stephen's spirit all around me. And on those days, life can go on. And there lies the reason for all these words of mine. My focus on the good stuff keeps him close in my heart and gives me strength for the coming days.

As a child, I coped in childlike ways. And now, years later, here I am with all those lessons in my pocket. Thank God for all of them, no matter how they arrived. If it hadn't been for my earlier adventures, I would not be coping with the loss of my son as I am today.

So, today's gratitude is for the past. It is because of it that I feel peace in my heart that everything will be okay, for I am resilient and open to learn more as the days pass.

I am deep today. It's the green tea and the washing machine. It makes me reflective. I can't wait for tomorrow. I'm going to drink orange juice and ask the microwave for advice.

January 12th: Stop the World, I Wanna Get Off for a While . . .

He that conceals his grief finds no remedy for it.

~Turkish Proverb~

One of the things I noticed shortly after Stephen died was the fact that the bills kept coming. For some reason, even though my world imploded, the electric company still felt like it was okay to charge me to keep the lights on. And even though my heart was broken, people were still mean or petty. The world continued to spin, and I could not find the emergency stop button.

I wanted to scream, "All I want is some peace! I need quiet because I am hurting!"

If I had it my way, I would have, instead of bills, received notes from the rest of the world saying something along the lines of:

Dear Kelly,
I know that life has just fallen apart. I know you can't imagine getting out of bed in the morning, let alone dealing with the day-to-day unkindness that exists in this world of ours. So, we'll take care of it. We want you to take a bath and read a book and take a nap. We want you to feel safe enough to let the world stop for a little bit, so you can properly grieve someone as wonderful as Stephen. So, take some time. We've got this covered. Know that we love you, and you live in the kind of world where we take care of each other in times like this.

Sincerely,

The Universe

I know that can't happen. But wouldn't it be nice if it could? Wouldn't it be nice if we understood that taking the time to grieve is really, really important? Wouldn't it be wonderful if we all took turns supporting each other through this process to make sure we made it through the journey okay?

Our culture has a time limit set on everything. In the corporate world, grieving is slated as a 3-day process according, to the Human Resources Department. Those who experience loss find that after a certain period of time, people don't want to talk about it. They will be told, as I have, that it is time to move on now. So, we who have lost try to fit into the society-accepted norms for grieving and then wonder why we don't feel good. We start to have physical symptoms, lean on unhealthy crutches for coping. And we have no idea why.

I can't get the utility companies to stop sending the bills. I can't stop the world from being wonky sometimes; I can't zap the mean and insensitive people with my laser, turning them into kind and gentle souls. But I can control how I live. And how I live will be measured in how I loved, so it is taking me longer than 3 days, thank you very much.

January 14th: The True Meaning of Winning . . .

By letting it go it all gets done. The world is won by those who let it go.
But when you try and try. The world is beyond the winning.

~Lao Tzu~

This weekend, we will be attending the Stephen Russell Memorial Tournament. I have to admit, it is a bit of a surreal feeling to be attending a tournament named in memory of your son. That's just not the way I envisioned things playing out. However, despite the feeling of melancholy about the reality of the situation, I am deeply touched and excited about the weekend. These boys have honored him in a way that has been so, so special and so comforting to me and my family. Words cannot articulate how they have positively impacted my grief.

I think Stephen would find the whole thing kind of embarrassing, although he would be honored. He would be surprised that he was getting this much attention and would not realize why. He didn't see the way he impacted people. I miss him so.

Hockey is a beautiful thing. I've said it before and will continue to sing its praises as a sport that breeds something beautiful into human beings. It is one based on history, respect, and tradition. As the mom of two goalies, I also know it is based on painstaking rituals. The sport has taught my children so much about life and the spirit of competition. They have learned firsthand about winning and losing. And they have collected all these lessons as they have glided around with blades on their feet, hoping to be struck by a frozen puck. My boys have taught me so much about the true meaning of winning.

Stephen's favorite game of hockey was a loss. He played the game in October 2007, against Florida Gulf Coast University (FGCU). The boys traveled down to Florida for a weekend of games. FGCU has a strong hockey program, and it shows in their results.

In any case, Stephen and the boys were ready for the game and up for the challenge. That night, there were thousands in attendance. NC State lost that game 4–1. I remember the call from Stephen that night. It was about 1:30 in the morning, and we were sound asleep. Fumbling in the darkness for the phone, Brady answered to hear Stephen on the other end.

After a particularly interesting game, no matter what the time of day, Stephen would call, and we would review every shot, every save, every penalty, every penalty kill, every goal and subtle nuance of the game. I loved those moments with him. He was *so* passionate about it. I remember before he died a person commenting on how intense he was when it came to hockey, it was like he was playing for the Stanley Cup. Now, looking back, I am glad he was intense. I am glad he left it all out on the ice and played like it was the Stanley Cup final. Because for him, it was.

Makes me think about what I should be more intense about in my own life. What if this is my game seven?[1]

Anyway, Brady and I reviewed the game with him, and I remember him saying at the end of the conversation, "Mom, we didn't win, but I gave it everything. And by the third period, the Florida Gulf Coast fans were chanting my name and cheering for me. It was so cool."

I could feel his joy across the phone lines, as this was "the game" he would remember as his best. And he lost. They lost the game.

---

[1] Game seven is the final game in a seven-game series. This game occurs in the postseasons for Major League Baseball (in the League Championship Series and World Series), the National Basketball Association (in all NBA playoff rounds), and the National Hockey League (in all Stanley Cup playoff rounds).

A few months ago, through a coincidence, we came in contact with one of the coaches of FGCU, who just happened to be one of the leaders of a hockey camp Brendan was attending. After speaking with us, he worked hard to find us the footage of "the game" and sent us the score sheet for us to see the amazing number of shots Stephen had saved. But the best part was what he said to us. Again, the power of simple words that we can carry with us, painting a beautiful memory of our boy:

"We here at FGCU Hockey extend our sincere sympathy for your loss. Although I don't remember each player on each opposing team, I do remember *our* fans cheering *your* son—a remarkable game, as he faced 54 shots!"

Winning has nothing to do with the score. It has everything to do with leaving it all out on the ice. Sure, it's nice to take home the gold, hoist the cup, and do the skate around. But a true win in life is the knowledge that you used everything that God gave you to try your best.

Today I am thankful that I have children that teach me every day about how I should be living my life.

January 21st: Going with the Flow of Change

The doors we open and close each day decide the lives we live.

~Flora Whittemore~

In my previous corporate life, I worked a lot with the concepts of change management. I don't feel like that person anymore, and sometimes I wonder if I will ever be able to go back to that type of work. In those days, I would apply the principles of change management to organizational restructuring within a company entity, attempting to close the gap between the old and new way of doing things. Sometimes it worked, and sometimes it really, really did not. You see, change management is not a sure thing. It is dependent on the people who are being asked to change and whether or not they want it.

One of my favorite illustrations of resistance to change comes from a meeting I facilitated a number of years ago. The changes to this organization were sweeping, and our team was trying to bring everyone into the conversation to see what role they would play in the company going forward. To bring some lighthearted humor to this meeting, we had hand-clapper party favors on each person's chair. If they liked what they heard, they could shake their party favor in the air and make the hands clap in approval. Was it corny? Yes. But we needed to get people out of their own heads long enough to see that some of these innovative ideas could work. Sometimes, acting silly is the best way to get people to let their guards down.

The attendees had a great time with it, and I felt so good as I watched the momentum building and moving towards consensus for the new operations. The meeting ended, and we received wonderful feedback. I felt satisfied that things were moving along in the right direction.

As the room emptied, I worked with my team to clean up the remnants of this daylong meeting. Picking up papers and things, I slowly moved from table to table. And then, sitting on one of the chairs, I found it. The plastic clapping hands. But the small plastic device was no longer the tool to spread positive energy. It has been modified by the person who was sitting here and left for us to find. The clapping hands had every finger cracked off except the middle one. Essentially, I had been "given the finger" by a set of red and yellow plastic clapping hands.

Thinking back to who had been sitting in this section, I knew immediately who had left me the one-fingered salute. He had been opposed to the change—any change, in fact—since the start. He had sat in the meeting and pouted all day, only stopping long enough to poke fun at others who were beginning to buy into the new way of doing things.

I never asked him about the hands; it would have served no purpose. Instead, I watched him over the next 3 months. As more people began to move forward, he continued to dig his heels in. Finally, he left the organization. I spoke to him prior to leaving, and what he said changed me forever. "I knew it wasn't going to work anyway. I'm glad to be leaving, because this place is going to hell in a hand basket."

Do you know why the change did not work out for him? He did not work with the change. He fought it and mocked it every step of the way. He made up his mind from the onset that it would not work. And guess what? He had been 100 percent right. He had created the outcome for himself.

So, why am I going on and on about change management? Because if there is one thing in life we can count on, it is change. I've thought about this a lot as I figure out who I am going to be in this next chapter of my life. And do you know what I know for sure? I don't want to be the girl who gives the finger to the universe because I don't like the cards that have been dealt to me.

I have read and believe that life should be looked at as a river, with ebbs and flows in the current, areas where the rocks are treacherous, rapids that take you for rides that are both thrilling and scary at the same time. The river is sometimes abundant and overflowing; at some points, the water's volume can dwindle, leaving you at a standstill and stagnant. But no matter what the river's makeup at any particular time, the way to succeed in life is to go with the flow of it. Swimming against the current of your life will never work and will only tire you physically and emotionally. Stick a paper boat in the stream. Does it ever turn around and come back? No. It keeps moving forward.

It does not seem right that I lost Stephen. But fighting it will not change it. Trying to swim upstream will not bring me back to him. Rather, I surrender to the current and see where this river will take me. It is changing me as a human being. I am still sad, but I am peaceful. And I am open to where the waterway takes me, knowing that change, whether good or bad, is part of the journey.

January 22nd: Che Sera, Sera

Che sera, sera,

Whatever will be, will be.

The future's not ours to see.

Che sera, sera.

~From the song written by Jay Livingston and Ray Evans~

Family. The way we live our own lives is tied to our roots in many ways. I can look over the past 6 and a half months and see that many of my ways of coping were given to me by my parents. They showed me how to be resilient in times of trouble. They showed me how to see the good in every situation. I am thankful that those are the lessons I have in my pocket.

But the lesson I carry with me more than anything is right there on my family crest. My family motto is:

"Che Sera Sera – Whatever Will Be, Will Be."

As for the rest of the crest, I am not too sure about the goat on the top, but I am sure it means something good, right?[2]

I can think of no better family motto for **The Resilient Russells**.

Whatever will be will be. The simple statement says it all. So, today, I am thankful for the roots that run deep in my family and keep me anchored as I journey through loss.

We're a loud and rambunctious group, but we love each other hard, and we stand together through whatever comes and learn to make it a part of the glorious fabric of our family.

---

[2] Goats actually symbolize sure-footedness, moving forward, and climbing to the top.

February 7th: The Rub

We must be willing to let go of the life we planned, so as to have the life that is waiting for us.

~Author Unknown ~

I've always been a girl who marched to my own drum. Even when I was younger and wanted desperately to fit into whatever group I thought would prove my worthiness, I knew my internal song was somewhat different. In fact, marching to my own drum does not describe it adequately. It felt more like I had my very own band. In my youth, I used to feel uncomfortable with my uniqueness. I looked at my differences as a negative rather than a positive. I lamented about those differences, changed the differences, and masked the differences. Essentially, for a long time, I swam against the current of my own life.

As the years passed and I had safely made the passage from youth to adulthood (fortunately, I've yet to grow up), I let go of most of these hang-ups. I created my own life, made peace with some things within it, and once I started to make the right choices, I began to hear the beauty in the music of my own drum.

So, imagine my surprise as I found myself, after all this self-work, questioning where I belong in life these days, in the big picture.

It has been 7 months since Stephen died. For much of this time, I have quietly lived a life of reflection. It is a life focused on my husband and son, and for the first time ever, I feel like it is a life of purpose. I write, I work, I do laundry, I reflect on where I came from and where I sit right now. It is life stripped bare, and it is simple to understand. I like it that way.

But, with the passage of each month on the calendar, I step back a little further into real life, whatever that means. This is where "The Rub" comes in.

This weekend, we were out and about, with hockey and life. As the weekend wore on, I could feel myself becoming fatigued with socialization. I was talking to people, and I could feel myself feeling, well, a little bitter, maybe even a touch angry. I was a little overwhelmed with the "regular" conversations, talking about the games or wins or losses or the petty annoyances of life. This has nothing to do with the other parents or what they were saying to me. More than that, it is what I found *myself* saying in an effort to be social and make conversation, rather than be the grieving woman sitting quietly in the corner reading my Pema Chödrön book.

I was pissing myself off. And ladies and gentlemen, that takes talent.

It was as if I was watching myself step back into the minutia of life, the regular, the life where we complain and moan just for something to do, where we talk about the easy things, what's on TV, who you're cheering for in the Super bowl, upcoming travel, play time. The life where we take the silly stuff too seriously and the real stuff too lightly. The life where we will lament for weeks about a coworker who gave us a "look" one day at a meeting, but we will not allow ourselves 5 minutes to contemplate why we have this underlying feeling of sadness, anger, or fear. I was upset with myself because I felt myself falling back into it.

And that felt awful. I was having this whole internal struggle about who I am now versus who I was 7 months ago. Brady took me outside, and we talked for a bit about my feelings. I was lamenting about why I was so different, why I couldn't be just comfortable to step back into my regular life.

And, as he began to speak to me, I realized I had married a guru.

He called it **"The Rub."** As he explained it to me, we have been living this very stripped-down life.

Every day, to survive, I focus on what is good and the love in our world and the positive that surrounds us. This is not optional for me. This is not a gratitude journal I purchased after watching a self-help DVD on how to transform your life in 30 days. No, this is gratitude that I aggressively search for, much like Indiana Jones searched for treasure in one too many sequels. My gratitude is not found easily some days; it is discovered with faith and determination. It is found with choice.

The Rub happens because I can feel the *old* life rub up against me, but I'm not that person anymore. And I can never go back to the way it was before. Now that time has passed and we are back into the routine of life, the Rub is more pronounced. Regular life rubs up against us with more frequency and intensity, and we feel compelled to respond to it. It is much like oil and water trying to mix. What I felt was not anger or bitterness; it was the Rub, reminding me that the person I have become since losing Stephen is different. And, as much as I thought so in high school, different is not a bad thing.

The Rub is telling me, "Don't forget or deny all that you've learned. The knowledge is too important. Don't fall back into the same thought patterns. Figure out how to make the lessons part of your new life." Today, I am thankful for The Rub.

February 14th: Pancakes, Chocolate, a Chimp in a Tutu, and Love

Love is a symbol of eternity. It wipes out all sense of time, destroying all memory of a beginning and all fear of an end.

~Madame de Staël~

Valentine's Day. The day of love and chocolate, where you snuggle up with chocolate and the person that gave you the chocolate.

Love and hurt. The two walk hand in hand, much like many of the couples celebrating today. How deeply we have loved is related to the depth of the hurt we experience when that love changes. They are connected, and one cannot exist without the other. That is life.

So, on this first February 14th without Stephen, I've selected a special few to "be my valentine":

Brendan – I am thankful for chocolate chip pancakes made with love. I am thankful for a two-foot-high Valentine's Day card from that same 12-year-old with a picture of a chimp in a tutu on the front. I am also thankful that he had to draw the Montreal Canadiens symbol on the front of that tutu because no occasion can be complete without the Canadiens or some hockey reference. I am thankful for the love that sits within his chest, who he is, and who he is becoming.

Stephen – Stephen taught me my first lessons about unconditional love. And my latest lessons about love were given to me by him and God. I did not make him a card or buy him chocolates, but I send my love to him today—in my words, in my actions, in my prayers. And as I look at the sunshine outside my window, the love that envelopes my home, and the gratitude that has found its way into my life, I feel his love too. Stephen shows me daily that love never dies.

Brady – My husband, my valentine. It seems like a logical choice. But this year, it is different. It is much deeper. As I sign his card this year, I not only think about our fun times together, our getting married on the beach, our romance and friendship. I think about him holding my hand and crying with me on July 5th. I think about him quietly making phone calls, making arrangements, travel reservations, finalizing funeral details. I think about him in the months following the funeral, protecting me, sheltering me from the world as I grieved and cried buckets of tears. I think about him doing that even though his heart was breaking too. I think about him carrying the burdens of our life so I could sit in my office and write. And finally, I think about what he gave Stephen. I can't put into words what they had together, but it was magic. It was unlikely, given the limited time they had with each other. But there it was. He showered him with this unconditional love and attention. And the best part? Stephen gave it right back to him. They created this joy in our house. And as I sign my husband's card this year, I do so knowing I will spend the rest of my life saying thank you for the love that filled Stephen's heart because of him.

Love does not die. It may change. It may not be as obvious as someone standing in front of you, but it never, ever dies.

February 28th: Tulips and Steaming Dog Crap

People who look through keyholes are apt to get the idea that most things are keyhole shaped.

~Author Unknown~

The tulips in the back bed have started to pop up. I am excited, because it has been an unusual winter here in the Carolinas—cold and more cold. The tulips are a sign of life from the cold ground, a good sign that spring will indeed come this year, despite the cold temperatures leading up to this moment.

I look at the tulips and think a little on how they represent life and the human spirit in so many ways. Over the past 8 months, I've experienced the winter of my life. And much like the bulbs beneath the ground, my quiet and painful winter is beginning to subside, and I am starting to feel ready for the sunshine on my face again.

I feel mighty proud as I reflect and look at the greenery shooting from the ground. Boy, I am deep and wise.

And then I see it.

In the corner of my eye, as I gaze on the tulips, I see rising steam. At first, I am confused, knowing that the dryer vent is on the other side of the house. But on closer inspection, I see it. Steaming on the ground, it is Rudy's own creation, left strategically in front of my window, so I may watch the steam billow up into the morning sky.

Gee, thanks, Rudy.

I laugh as I look at the two focal points from this different perspective. And then I realize. Rudy has unknowingly completed the picture. Did I mention he is a Wonder Dog?

Life is like the tulip for me, new life emerging, slowly and tentatively, not knowing what will happen when you break through to the other side. My life and the tulip endure, even though we may only show our beauty and bravery with the right season and retract when it gets too cold and unbearable. Life and the tulip are meant to be lived, even in the harshest of circumstances. I think about the tulip bulb beneath the ground, living life within a contained shell that would ensure its survival, and it sounds like how I have been living since Stephen's death—protecting my broken heart, living in my shell for months. But as with the tulip, I knew, in my broken heart, that I would find a way to blossom once again.

Truly, real life is more like the complete picture I see out my window, with Rudy's oh-so-generous addition to the canvas.

You can reemerge from the winter of your life as a tulip. But no matter what you've been through or how hard the winter was, when you reemerge, there it is.

Crap.

Crap is a part of life. No matter how you try to change it, you will always have the balance of good and bad in life. There will always be people and situations that will hurt you, anger you, irritate, and raise your blood pressure.

The key to happiness is in how you look at it.

I like to think of life as a photograph, and I am the photographer. As the photographer, what do I see through my lens? The tulip? Or the steaming dog crap? Will I be so disgusted that Rudy ruined the picture that I lose sight of the tulip completely? Or worse, do I throw my hands up in the air and say, "There's no point in taking the picture, because it's not perfect!"

I choose to realize that the balance of the two is what makes the tulip more beautiful. I choose to see the miracle of the tulip, being able to break through the cold ground and exist even though the environment may not be perfect for its survival. I choose to focus my lens on the tulip and realize that Rudy's contribution will eventually serve as fertilizer to make next year's blooms more colorful and resilient.

Life is all in how you look at it. A life lived well is a life that understands that the good and the bad go together, and both are our teachers on the journey.

March 5th: Pecking at the Kick Plate of Life

*Be as a bird perched on a frail branch that she feels bending beneath her,
still she sings away all the same, knowing she has wings.*

~Victor Hugo~

The birds are back. I love to both watch and listen to them in the
yard. They are a melodic reminder of the coming warmth, and I am
all for that.

But Mr. Robin is having issues. For the past few weeks, Mr. Robin
has been coming to my front door every morning and pecking at the
kick plate at the base of the door. He stands there, and for at least 10
minutes a day, he essentially bangs his head against the door. I've
analyzed the situation and have come to the conclusion that he is
playing the dating game. Although I am no expert in the behavior
patterns of birds, I think he sees his reflection in the kick plate and
is making advances on himself in the hopes of procreation.

And how's that working out for him?

For the first few days, Rudy would stand at the door and growl and
scratch at the floor, as if he was sending a message to the bird. I
would go to the door and gently knock at the base until he flew
away. I just could not bear to think this cute creature was going to
have a head injury because of his desire to find a mate. After a few
weeks of this, Rudy gave up. It was as if he said, "Okay, guy, you
want to bang your head against the door? Fill your boots. I will be
lying on my leather couch. I'm done trying to talk sense to you."

I gave up too, fatigued from jumping from my office chair every
time I heard the noise at the base of the door.

How many times have I acted like the robin at one point or another in life? Day after day, we come back to the same place and bang our heads against the wall, expecting to get a different result. Days, weeks, months, and years pass, and all we have to show for it is a headache and no progress, no forward movement in our lives. We look at our own reflection, and that is the only part of the picture we see. We only see *our* story. We never turn away from the kick plate of life and see that there is a big world out there, waiting for us to participate and contribute our talents. We get stuck in our old patterns of thinking and worrying and assuming we have it all figured out. And with every bang against the door, we convince ourselves that we were right, that there is nothing else out there for us.

And just like the robin, we have people who approach us and gently say, "Ahem, excuse me? Did you know you're banging your head against the wall? May I suggest a better approach?"

And many times, how do we respond? Just like the robin. "This is my head and my reflection, and I feel comfortable banging my head every day, thank you very much. I am scared to turn around and see the real world, so I will continue to do what I know and that is to injure myself. Now, leave me alone. My head hurts too much to talk to you!"

And slowly, the people drift away. They tried, and they failed, so they move on, and leave you to your head-banging. Much like Rudy and myself, they move on, because it appears you don't want to be helped. If Mr. Robin turned away from the kick plate and instead looked for a live *Ms.* Robin, what would he get? Woohoo! Candlelit dinners, movies, long walks home, and some mini robins in the spring. If only he knew that the unknown was so much better than the kick plate. His resistance is holding him back from the beautiful possibilities of life. Today I am thankful for Mr. Robin. He is teaching me that I need to take a deep cleansing breath and turn around. The world is waiting . . .

March 8th: How to Parent Like a Deer in the Headlights

The best inheritance a parent can give his children is a few minutes of time each day.

~O. A. Battista~

I love to watch Brendan play hard, both on and off the ice. I can see the smile comes more freely these days, and it makes me exhale a little. For many of my days, his smile has been my one little thing for the day. When Stephen died, I wondered if I would see that spontaneous smile again, on his face or my own. As a mother, there is nothing more difficult than facing the fact that there are some hurts in life you can't protect your babies from. Sometimes, things happen, and you can support them and love them through it, but you just can't change it.

That is one of the hardest things for me to accept.

In the early days of our hurt, we would discuss some high-level things about what had happened, but honestly, most of the time, we simply looked at each other through our tear-filled eyes. We had this unspoken conversation of hurt and longing for his brother to be back with us. We held each other quietly and could only say simple things like,

"I miss him. I miss Stephen."

At night, I would pray for God to take away the pain he felt and give it to me tenfold, if only to spare him a small portion of the anguish. But that could not be the case, and he had to go on his journey just as I had to go on mine. And our journey continues.

I've tried to walk a mile in Brendan's shoes, to really reflect on what he has lost. Stephen was the best of big brothers, and he loved Brendan hard, without condition. Stephen spoke honestly to Brendan, gave him advice on everything from hockey skills to table manner to video games to life. It was the kind of advice that could only be given by a big brother and would only be accepted by Brendan if Stephen was the sender. When Stephen would come home on break from school, much of his time was focused on hanging with Brendan, laughing, giggling, wrestling, playing video games, taking off for some big adventure, stepping on the ice together. It was a special bond, and then everything changed.

I am trying so damn hard, but I can't change that. I can't make things go back to the way they were. It's just not fair.

When Stephen died, we were all left with so many questions. So many things we just needed 5 more minutes with him to clarify, to explain, to give us peace. Sadly, that could not happen, and we had to either find the answers on our own or make peace with the unknown. We continue to work on that daily.

I need to be honest. I feel hopelessly inadequate with my parenting skill set to handle this. Brendan asks tough, hard-hitting, investigative, reporter-type questions, and most of the time I find myself standing in front of him with a mouth gaping open, sweaty palms, and a look that resembles a deer in the headlights. I have this bright, intelligent, and thoughtful child, and for that I am grateful and blessed. But when he wants answers, stand back.

But no matter how sweaty my palms get when he asks a question with no answer, I am thankful. I am thankful that we are both learning that we can continue to live and learn and laugh—even if we don't have all the answers.

March 11th: Choosing Happiness

The foolish man seeks happiness in the distance, the wise grows it under his feet.

~James Oppenheim~

I am pathetic. I am trying to show Brendan that we can have this happy life, and I feel like the biggest fraud on the planet. But I keep trying.

Nike said it best: "Just do it." I put on my sneakers and jacket, and I go and cheer him on at a hockey game. I put on my hat and mittens and go outside with him and make a snowman from the freshly fallen white stuff in the Carolinas. I dance in the kitchen. I sing. I tickle. We have belly laughs as we watch Rudy drag his butt across the living room carpet. We simply choose happiness. Or at least that's what I try to convince him we're doing. Convince him *and* myself.

It is difficult some days to do it, to choose to smile when I want to cry. But I have a responsibility. I have a job to do. And that job is to show my son that life is made up of cycles and that the "recipe" includes both good and bad. And it is the combination of the two that makes our time here so magical, delicious, painful, and touching. It is the combination that makes life worth living. A storm pours rain from the heavens, but eventually, the clouds clear and the sun returns. The flowers bloom because of the rain. Night falls, and the darkness may make us afraid, but the morning comes— always.

The way I see it, I have to teach Brendan that it is okay to return to happiness. I have to show him that returning to joy after sadness is *part of life*. It is not an option for us to stay sad forever. We will always miss Stephen and long for him to still be with us, of course. But life is meant to be lived. And living can only be called living if you approach it with wild abandon and joy.

Imagine if we didn't let the happiness back in . . . I would finally get to the end of my days, and I would see Stephen again, and he would say, "Now why did you go and let yourself waste all that living and laughing and learning and loving? You died right along with me."

No, sir. Can't do that. I have a 12-year-old who is entitled to a world filled with laughter and silliness and joy. So, even if I feel like a fraud, I will keep trying.

Today I am thankful for the glorious moments of happiness I have each and every day with my boy. As the laughter swirls around our house, I can almost hear Stephen laughing with us, cheering us on and urging us to keep living large.

March 16th: Each Name is a Stephen to Someone

Die when I may, I want it said by those who knew me best that I always plucked a thistle and planted a flower where I thought a flower would grow.

~Abraham Lincoln~

We traveled to Washington, DC, for the last hockey tournament of the season. It was great hockey, but we also took some time to see some of the sites of Washington, as Brendan and I are still learning about this new country of ours. Our time was limited, but we managed to see the White House, the Lincoln Memorial, the Vietnam Veterans Memorial, the World War II Memorial, the Korean War Memorial, and the Washington Monument. I was so impressed with all of it, and we have already discussed returning when we have more time to explore some more of this amazing city.

But in a way, I am glad that my viewing was limited to the memorials. What makes a life memorable, why is it important to remember, and what happens when we don't? What about the guys who are remembered long after they are dead and gone? What made them memorable?

As I stood at the base of Abe sitting in his big old chair pondering whatever you ponder when you are Abraham Lincoln, I could not help but think about why a monument of this magnitude would be built. Walking further down the mall and looking at the memorials to the Vietnam Veterans and World War II, I was again moved by the power of remembrance.

They were all created to remember lives devoted to service and sacrifice to a country and its people. But they all evoked different emotions for me. Lincoln left me with a feeling of inspiration, even motivation, for what can be accomplished when a person sets their mind to a task with humility and a focus on what is right. The World War II Memorial was one of pride and celebration for those who had paid the ultimate price for victory. But the Vietnam War Veterans Memorial was overwhelming. The very wall oozed with emotion, and the pain was palpable. It was raining, and as I watched the drops drizzling down on the wall, I felt they could be tears, still falling from time to time on this wall to remind the visitors of the loss. For me, each one showed respect and reverence for those lost but in vastly different ways. Each one evoked emotions that were at both ends of the spectrum. And it got me thinking. How am I remembering my lost loved ones? How would I like to be remembered?

As Brendan and I stood at the entry to the Vietnam War Veterans memorial, we quietly talked for a few moments about what it represented. Close to the entrance to the monument, there is a bronze sculpture of three soldiers, standing much as they would in a field somewhere preparing for battle. The faces are haunting, and as you look closely at the detail, you feel they could start a conversation with you at any moment. Brendan and I looked at them for a long time. He asked thoughtful questions about the war and the reasons for the war, and I am afraid my answers were not at all academic or enlightening.

But when we spoke about what this and the other memorials meant, I told him the truth. Every name on this wall is a "Stephen" to someone. There is a mother or a brother or a dad or a friend who loves these people just like we love Stephen. Wars will come and go, and people will forget what they were fighting about, but the one thing that always remains is how we loved.

We walked quietly past the names, reverent and respectful. Brendan stopped and spoke to the National Park Service employees, asking questions that were well beyond his years. We paused and looked at the pictures in Zip-loc bags, laid at the base of the wall, colored carefully with crayons by an elementary school class to give thanks to soldiers they never knew.

And even if it was only for an instant, we felt the pain of the wall. We felt the hurt and the loss.

I am humbled and a little ashamed to admit that prior to losing my own son, I probably would have walked through and reflected for only an instant on the loss. I would have been in awe at the construction of the monuments themselves but would not have spent time thinking about what they represented.

But now, I am different. And that is a good thing.

I am a more compassionate human being, and for that, I am grateful.

Because each name on that wall is a Stephen to someone.

March 18th: The Day the Music Died

Were it not for music, we might in these days say, the Beautiful is dead.

~Benjamin Disraeli~

I received a note from a former music teacher who was kind enough to check in with me. Her last words were to say that she hopes I'm still singing. It's funny, because I find myself many times throughout my day looking for comfort within music—finding the right tunes, the right words to make me feel connected, to elicit memories about Stephen, to motivate me to keep moving, no matter how small the step. The songs speak the language of my heart, saying what I cannot convey in simple conversation.

But although I listen to music and it has been a faithful companion, I have not been able to sing since Stephen died. I used to be this girl who would, at some point every day, sneak away, and pick up my guitar and sing something. Every single day. And then, as Don McLean so aptly put it, the music died.

I feel as if the music left my heart, and my vocal cords have been removed. I can only manage to listen, never sing along. Sometimes, as I listen, I even want to sing, but nothing comes.

I realize that I cannot sing, because my music comes from deep within my heart, and that heart is broken open.

Each month, I will continue to dust off my guitars and look at my music books. And wonder when I will ever be able to pick them up again. Perhaps one day in the future, the music will return. I hope for that day, because when I sing, I feel more alive, and in many ways, it feels like praying. Someday, the music will return to my heart.

So, today, I give thanks for the people who continue to make music in my absence. Their melodies tell a story that I cannot quite tell myself just yet. They are my voice and my reminder that the music is still there. Because one day, I will sing again.

Alas for those that never sing, but die with all their music in them!

~Oliver Wendell Holmes~

March 22nd: Is There a Dress Code in Heaven?

Heaven wheels above you, displaying to you her eternal glories, and still your eyes are on the ground.

~Dante Alighieri~

It's been a tough few days; I'm not sure why, it just was another point on the trail where the reality of all of this struck me. He did not come home for spring break, and he is not getting ready to graduate. And I just broke open all over again as I thought about it. Because he was just so special, and it makes me so sad when I think about all the dreams of what he could have done in this world. The tears flow freely as I write, I need some sort of protective covering over my laptop.

When I am really missing Stephen, I wonder about where he is. I wonder about heaven. People talk about heaven like it is this fluffy cloud with harps and angels, with God having a beautiful melodic and seasoned voice like Morgan Freeman. But truly, we don't know. In the 8 months since Stephen's death, I have explored every aspect of my faith, from what I believe about God to what I believe about heaven. And there is still much I will not understand until it is time for me to know. But I am trying my absolute best to have faith.

In that time, I've read books, mainstream and controversial. I've explored religions, all sorts, from Buddhism to my own Catholicism and every version of Christianity in between, searching for some . . .. . definitive answer? Proof? An emailed confirmation number that Stephen arrived safely?

Have I found confirmation of heaven? No. But, as each month passes, God shows me that he is looking out for me and wiping away the tears and showing me the way through this. God is showing me with each word I type that I will be okay. I believe I am being shown I will be more than okay; I will be a better person because of this hurt. With every version of organized religion, I have explored, I have found a little piece of the truth for me.

I don't know where heaven exists or the guidelines for admission or the dress code. I don't know what the lines are like or if there is a waiting area or if you need to pack a lunch. I don't know if there is purgatory like Sister Georgina mentioned in second grade, but I have to say, if there is, I've got some work to do. I don't know. But what I do know is this: I have faith it is all the good things I imagine, where all the wonderful people whom I have lost are right now.

March 24th: A Little Piece of Heaven on Earth

Earth's crammed with heaven, and every common bush afire with God;
But only he who sees, takes off his shoes; The rest sit round it and pluck
blackberries . . .

~Elizabeth Barrett Browning~

I paid a visit to Jordan Lake today. I felt compelled to return to the spot where I stood in the early morning hours of July 5th. I cried as I watched the glistening water in that quiet cove, and I talked to Stephen. It was the first time I had returned to that place, and it seemed fitting that it was in the spring of the year, with life beginning to bloom again. It's a beautiful place, and I know that may seem weird for me to say about the place where my son died. But it is. It is peaceful and beautiful and reverent.

As I walked back up the trail, I saw a blanket of forget-me-nots growing on the side of the hill, the same flowers Stephen planted with me in our back flower bed 2 years before because they were one of my mother's favorites.

No, Stephen, I will not forget you, and I hope that with each step I take, I continue to honor the magnificent human being you were.

So, what am I thankful for today? I am thankful for the serene cove and the fact that I choose to see its beauty rather than the event that happened here, forever changing my life.

And I am thankful for Stephen. I am thankful that the impact of his life is having a bigger ripple effect than I could ever have imagined.

God, thank you for this full circle kind of day. It has reminded me that we don't need to wait to see heaven. There are pieces of it right here on earth, in front of us, angels and all. We only have to look for them.

March 26th: God's Special Reel of Film . . .

I wonder whether they have rum and Coke in Heaven. Maybe it's too mundane a pleasure, but I hope so—as a sundowner. Except, of course, the sun never goes down there. Oh, man, this heaven is going to take some getting used to.

~Desmond Tutu~

Well, Friday has finally arrived. It has been an emotional week with my prayers at water's edge, and I'm just missing Stephen so, so much. The visit has reminded me of some of the lessons bestowed upon me at water's edge on that wet July morning, lessons about living life versus getting through life.

With that in mind, I took some time today to write this story. I don't know why, but I feel I may be right about heaven.

You see the light. You can't believe it. The end has come, and you cross over to the other side. Heaven. It is everything you imagined and more, and the faces of the people who greet you are welcoming and filled with love. You see the gates ahead and begin to walk with your loved ones towards the entrance. The worries from your earthly life begin to fade, and although you will miss those left behind, you are happy to be here.

But as you approach the entrance gates, you see the ropes are up, guiding you into a theatre instead of through the gates. A beautiful angel sits next to you and passes you some popcorn, buttered of course, because cholesterol is not an issue in heaven. You are confused. It makes no sense. This is not the time for movies. This is the time to get in through gates and see the magnificence of God's heaven.

Sensing your discomfort, the angel touches your hand and tells you not to worry. The movie is part of your welcome. Everyone has to watch it before entering, and each movie is individual to your life. God has made yours special just for you.

The lights dim, and the movie begins. Scenes of your life flash before you — hugs from your mother, the giggles of your childhood, your first kiss, holding your child in those first moments after birth. Favorite songs and food and people flash across the screen, and with each glimpse, you remember the emotion of the moments. You watch with tear-filled eyes the moments of your life where you were brought to your knees in pain, the moments where life crushed you into the ground, then stepped on you a second time to make sure you could never be put back together quite the same way again. You think to yourself that God saw it all, and you marvel at the fact that He was with you on the entire journey.

But then the movie takes a turn and begins to show you scenes of your life that are not familiar. Scenes with so much love and happiness. You look at your own face on the screen and you don't really recognize yourself. There are scenes that show you helping others, changing lives, living your purpose, and making a difference. You tug on the sleeve of the angel's robe and say there must be some mistake. This is not your movie, it is someone else's.

*And the angel responds, "No, this is your life. This is just **God's special reel** of film. This is how God envisioned it, not how you lived it."*

*So, you watch with wonder. And you see what life would have been **if**:*

Instead of anger, you had decided to love, without condition or expectation.

Instead of judging, you had decided to be tolerant of everyone, no matter what the differences.

Instead of bitterness, you had decided to forgive.

Instead of fear, you decided to be fearless and trust that God really did have your back.

And because of those simple decisions, you lived *more of your life, instead of* living through *it.*

You watch quietly, amazed at how different things could have been with some simple choices.

The curtain closes and the lights come back on, and you look to the angel and ask, "Can I go back and try this over? I know I can do better."

The angel replies, "No, and God did not show you those scenes to make you fill with regret. He showed you so you could understand. Life is and always will be about the love. God showed you this, because he intends to show pieces of this to those you left behind on earth as well. In their dreams and through their hurt, your life will teach them. And maybe, if they are not afraid and open their hearts to see the message through the pain, they can choose differently because of what you and He taught them. And when it is their time, maybe God's special reel for them will be a bit shorter."

I guess I need to start asking myself what I'm leaving on the cutting room floor.

Today, I am thankful for my imagination and my decision to not leave any more film on the cutting room floor.

April 1st: The Blown Engine

The one thing you can't take away from me is the way I choose to respond to what you do to me. The last of one's freedoms is to choose one's attitude in any given circumstance.

~Victor Frankl~

We picked up Stephen's car today. It's been in storage since last spring, kept by a kind man who had no idea he would be taking care of it for this long. Last April, Stephen called us to say the car was having major issues, and boy, was he was right. Not long after the call, it died completely. I remember the night Brady and Stephen towed it from Raleigh. I looked at this broken piece of metal, thinking about how many dollars it was going to cost to get a new engine. The economy was in the toilet, and our business had slowed to what I describe as "short of breath." It was a scary time for everyone financially.

But when Stephen got out of the car, it did not matter to me. The money would be found somehow. And I hugged into him and said, "The car is toast, but on the upside, I get a surprise visit from you."

And he hugged me back, so tight. We hung out and laughed that night, and the next morning, before he left to go back to school, we sat for over an hour on the back deck and just talked about life and love and school and faith. And as he left, I felt so, so good because he was in such a good place. And he was no longer a boy. He was a man, a beautiful and thoughtful, intelligent, caring man. It was one of the last deep chats we had about life, laughing together in the spring sunshine.

That chat on the back deck sparked a series of emails that I held onto in the early days of my grief and actually played a huge role in shifting my focus on gratitude as I mourned his loss.

I forgot about those moments until the instant I saw the car. And when I looked at her (Xena is her name. I was told this by his friends, but I am not entirely sure of the story behind it, and not sure I *want* to know), I cried. All the memories of that day and so many more flooded my mind.

We thanked the man for watching over Xena until we were ready to pick her up. And we took her home. And when Brendan saw the car, he immediately went to it and looked in every compartment. I did too. The CDs were unchanged; his stuff was still in there. Brendan found his sunglasses and his cologne and was thrilled to find "Stephen's smell." We found lists and papers and cleaning supplies. All neatly organized. Brendan told us we must not change anything in there, not yet. Cue broken heart here.

It was like he had just parked in the driveway himself, and at any moment, would come around the corner. But he didn't. And I quietly went inside and cried the sobs that I have so many times before over the last 9 months. It just hurts, and there is no denying it.

We're keeping the car. Xena stays, and Brendan is thrilled to know that she waits for him when he finally gets his learner's permit.

So, what am I possibly thankful for today?

The blown engine. Without it, I would not have had that wonderful chat with him on the deck. I would not have heard the beautiful things that he said about life, love, and his faith and our relationship. I would not have been able to watch him and Brady, laughing and hugging in the driveway, smiling at a blown engine when others would have been cursing the sky. If it were not for the blown engine, I would not have had the email exchanges with him, sparking my gratitude in the face of loss that saved me.

And because of the blown engine, yesterday, for an instant, I felt him again, like he was just around the corner. I could feel his life as he'd left it. Today, I am thankful for a blown engine. It gave me a beautiful moment with my child I will cherish forever, and it gave us one last glimpse of life as he'd left it, confirming once again he was as amazing as I thought he was.

Thankful through tears but thankful just the same.

April 12th: The Power of Thoughts

Our Best friends and our worst enemies are our thoughts. A thought can do us more good than a doctor or a banker or a faithful friend. It can also do us more harm than a brick.

~Frank Crane~

I never thought I would be one of those people who counts the months without him. But I do. Nine months. And with each month's passing, I am becoming more acutely aware of the following:

My thoughts affect my emotions.

My emotions determine my actions or reactions.

My actions determine if it is going to be a good day or a bad day.

My days grow into weeks, then months, and all of those moments will be known as my life.

So, if I want to have a good life, I need to pay attention to those thoughts of mine. The quote I found today sums it up perfectly for me. We can use our thoughts as our greatest ally or our worst enemy. It is all entirely up to us.

I used to be the worst-case scenario girl. It was all very dramatic really, as I could take a simple situation with minimal risk and turn it into a sequel for Armageddon. I'm not sure how that all started in my life, but I think it had something to do with wanting to control my circumstances. I wanted to feel like I had it all figured out, along with any potential ripple effect that could come from a situation. I needed to feel a sense of control and thought that controlling the external circumstances in my life would give me peace.

And then, Stephen died, and I realized I was not in control at all. *Groundless* is a word used to describe it when all is stripped away. I've often said it is like the rug being pulled out from beneath your feet, and you tap your foot around feverishly looking for stability, only to find out the floor is gone too. It was the scariest time of my life, and at moments, I still have flashes of terror when I think about all that has transpired.

But you know what it taught me? Really, truly, the only thing I can have control over in my life is my thinking. I am the only person who can control my thoughts. I can make them positive or negative. I can look at my life and see someone who has nothing but bad luck, or I can see a life that is filled with blessings. That is why I write and find gratitude.

I choose happiness. I choose to look for and see the blessings in life. My thoughts don't take away the pain, but they make it easier to bear. Thinking thoughts of love and gratitude don't make me miss him any less, but they do allow me to see how blessed I was to have him for at least 23 years. They do allow me to see all that his short life has contributed to others.

In my oncology nursing days, I got to know the most amazing man, being the person who administered his chemotherapy for about 6 months. He was in his late seventies and had lived a life that was rich and full of travel and experiences. I always marveled at him, as he would skip into the cancer clinic where I worked, kind of like a kid rushing into a candy store. He had a loving and doting wife, and they acted as if they were teenagers still dating. Each week, I would sit and chat with him, and as the months passed, I could see that he was not getting better. He was slowly dying. He knew it, and so did his wife. But each week, they would arrive smiling. One day, when his wife left the room for a moment, he leaned over to me and said something along the lines of this:

"I know what's coming, but what good is talking and thinking about it going to do me? So, I made peace with it, and I am going to spend the rest of my time just living."

And he did. He realized that even though the circumstances were dire, he was in control of his thoughts. And he chose to be happy in his last days. He could have made excuses and given himself a free pass to complain because he was dying. But he chose to be happy, even in his last days, as he endured chemotherapy and the pain of his cancer.

I think about him from time to time, as he impacted my life and, in some ways, affected how I grieve for Stephen. And he never knew it.

Today I am thankful for him and for all the other people I have met on my journey who have given me the courage to live a life of gratitude. Today I am thankful that I keep telling myself that everything is going to be okay even when I don't quite believe it. Today I am thankful that I am paying attention to my internal self-talk.

Thoughts become emotions, emotions become actions, actions become days, and days become one's life. Today I am thankful for that knowledge and grateful that I am creating a happy life. Dr. Seuss said it best:

You have brains in your head. You have feet in your shoes. You can steer yourself any direction you choose. You're on your own. And you know what you know. You are the guy who'll decide where to go.

~Dr. Seuss~

April 28th: Pancakes, Teenagers, and Embracing Life's Joy

Because time itself is like a spiral, something special happens on your birthday each year: The same energy that God invested in you at birth is present once again.

~Menachem Mendel Schneerson~

Today is Brendan's 13th birthday. A day worth celebrating, we began with the breakfast of champions, pancakes shaped in the number 13. I'm not sure why, but I have to begin days of celebration with theme-shaped pancakes. For St. Paddy's, we have green shamrocks. I've done Christmas trees and letters and hearts. And for each birthday, I create a pancake that is the number of my child's age on that particular day. This was one of the toughest years yet, as I needed two spatulas to flip the number three.

I'm not sure what it says about a person when they express love and occasions in pancake batter. But I think it is good. I think it shows "you're worth the effort."

I smiled and waved as he left to catch the bus, belly full but still muttering something about how no child should have to go to school on his birthday.

And as I closed the door to begin my day, I noticed something. My heart felt light and good and joyful.

Nine months ago, I never thought I would have joy in my heart, ever again. I was convinced that I was not destined for a life of happiness and joy. But slowly, bit by bit, the happiness is starting to come back. The dark days of grief are starting to ease up, although I still have moments where I simply can't believe that this is my new reality.

I believe that happiness came back to me because I invited it in. I believe it resides in my heart because I have allowed it to do so. And when you lose someone as wonderful as Stephen, it is not always easy to do that, to let the joy back in. But I am so glad I did.

I did it bit by bit, moment by moment. I did it by appreciating a flower in bloom or a cuddle from my child or a memory of Stephen. I found joy in the kindness shown to me by friends and strangers alike, the unwavering support of my family, and my faith. I found joy because I looked for it. I made a choice to find it.

Brendan and I had a wonderful discussion about events like birthdays, wondering if it was okay to be happy on those days, even when we felt a little sad because Stephen was not physically with us.

And we both came to the same conclusion when we asked ourselves this question: **"What would Stephen want?"**

We both agreed that Stephen would want us to grab onto all the joys of life with two hands. We believe he would want us to drink up happiness and savor each breath of each day, not just the birthdays and graduations and parties. We know he would want us to choose happiness and live the life that God gave us with a "Game Seven of the Stanley Cup Final" mentality.

So, we will. Today, I am thankful for number-shaped pancakes, made each year with love for both of my boys. I am thankful for my beautiful boy, who awoke this morning and was still the sweet boy from the night before and had not transformed into a "scary teenager" as he slept. And I am thankful for the guidance that Stephen gives us every day, quietly leading us towards a joyful life.

May 3rd: The River of Tears

Delicious tears! The heart's own dew.
~Letitia Elizabeth Landon~

May is a tough one for me. I realized it would be one day in February, when the month of May suddenly jumped out at me in the calendar. In March, I felt a sense of dread when I thought about May, with all of its spring beauty and promise for a fabulous summer. And then, the month arrived, with no fanfare, just creeping in quietly, reminding me of the swift passage of time.

May is Stephen's birthday month. He would be 24 years old this year. May is the month he was supposed to graduate from NC State University and begin the next chapter of his life. May is the month, that just one year earlier, he was bounding up the stairs and laughing with Brendan, laughing and living life and completing our family.

May is a trigger month for me. I knew it would be, and I was right.

Today I am thankful for tears. There's so many of them, I may as well be thankful for them.

May 8th: Remembering My Mother Madge

I remember my mother's prayers and they have always followed me. They have clung to me all my life.

~Abraham Lincoln~

Mother's Day. I feel sad each year as this special day approaches, as my mother died in 1991. I've been thinking about her and about how I feel as a mother this year with my son in heaven.

It has been 20 years since the last Mother's Day I had with her. This is the tipping point, for next year, I will have spent more Mother's Days with her in heaven than with her on earth.

I can't even remember how we celebrated that last one. I have a feeling that I tried to get a good card, because in my awkward youth, I always relied on Hallmark to say what I couldn't quite articulate. She was so sick, and although I don't remember how we celebrated that year, I remember the feeling that I had as I realized she was slowly slipping away.

As the years have passed, I have quietly remembered her in my own way but not talked about it much, because to be honest, it was easier to push the pain away than stare it in the face. I have thought of her often on my grief journey, wishing for her presence with me as I cried my tears of loss. Everyone needs their mother when they hurt.

But as I have learned that grieving with gratitude can heal your heart, I've decided to celebrate my mom this year, in the same way I have celebrated Stephen since last July. With thanks . . .

Madge, this is for you . . ..

My Mom's legacy is about the simple gifts that a mother gives her children. Because, as you know, it is the simple gifts that are truly the most important in this life:

She was the best cook and could put flavor on a rock. She made the best homemade bread, and her coconut and sweet milk cookies were the stuff of legends. Each one of her children has perfected at least one of her recipes. Each Christmas, I think of her as I make my own "Christmas soup."

She was such a lady, the way she walked and presented herself with grace, no matter what the circumstance. She had these scarves and this long coat, and she lived her entire life without ever wearing a pair of jeans. She taught me about dignity and respecting others.

When she laughed, she did it with full commitment. Her head swung back, she slapped her leg and stomped her foot, and she made this lilting sound with her voice that sounded like a cross between singing and a hiccup. Her sisters laughed the same way, and I can remember being a kid on a sweltering summer day, sitting on the back step eating an orange Mr. Freeze and listening to all of them laugh, sitting in the lawn chairs in the sun enjoying their brief time together.

She was an expert hugger. She could hug you and shut out the rest of the world. She just made you feel that everything was going to work out, because she was squeezing the trouble right out of you. She had this intensity about her when she hugged people, almost as if she understood how fleeting life was, and if this was to be the last, she wanted to make it a good one. Her hugs . . . were amazing. If I could have bottled them and sent them all over the world, we would have world peace.

She taught me about unconditional love. She loved my dad and her children with a white-hot intensity and was fiercely protective of our family. She loved us and would tell us, even when we did not deserve to hear it sometimes. Sometimes, her expressions of love were not conveyed with words but quiet actions. The day I came to her as a teenager and told her I was pregnant with Stephen, she was getting ready to go out, and when the news was dropped in her lap, she threw her beige high heels at the refrigerator. Years later, as I think about that moment, I realize that in many ways, she was saying she loved me right then, because she didn't throw the shoes at me.

She showed me how to love my own children, and I've always thought of her as I praised and cheered my own boys, remembering the look on her face as she watched me sing in the Kiwanis Music festival.

She showed all of us the importance of family and how nothing should ever come between the bonds you have.

She nourished my faith and showed me an example of her own daily. She taught me that true faith, true Christianity happens not only in a pew on Sunday but every day in how you treat the people who cross your path.

She slammed the cupboard doors when things displeased her, and now, as I am a mother myself, I think about that every time I lose my cool. (I slam doors, by the way.)

She, more than anyone else on this earth, showed me how to be resilient. My mother showed me how to bounce back and how to steer your ship back on course when a storm threatens to throw you against the jagged coastline. She was a master navigator, although she never realized it when she was alive.

She showed me that just because life is not perfect, it doesn't mean you can't live a perfect life. My mother showed me the art of making life good and making the best of any situation.

I realized after she passed that she was the magic that made Christmas a holiday, a birthday worth celebrating, Easter eggstra special. She set the table and went the extra mile to show you it all mattered. She showed me the importance of making the extra effort and making life special.

Today, I am thankful for my magic mother. I hope she's giving Stephen one of her legendary hugs right about now.

May 9th: The Only Gift I Need on Mother's Day

A mother is the truest friend we have, when trials heavy and sudden fall upon us; when adversity takes the place of prosperity; when friends who rejoice with us in our sunshine desert us; when trouble thickens around us, still will she cling to us, and endeavor by her kind precepts and counsels to dissipate the clouds of darkness, and cause peace to return to our hearts.

~Washington Irving~

Sunday mornings. I love to sneak away and write a few lines before the day begins, and Mother's Day is no different.

And on this Sunday, I have lots to say. As a result of my "stare at the ceiling" thoughts this morning, I have lots to say about my first Mother's Day without Stephen.

May is tough for me for a variety of reasons. So, as this day was fast approaching, I fell into the trap of focusing on a Mother's Day without him.

On my first Mother's Day, I felt too young and inadequate to deserve the accolades that were reserved for people as terrific as my own mother.

I remember a Mother's Day when Stephen was a young boy. He was sprinting towards his school knapsack to pull out the most amazing creation he had made for me at school. It would be wrinkled and covered with crumbs of unknown origin from sitting in the bottom of his bag. But he would shake it off and thrust it towards me like I was an award winner at the Oscars.

And finally, I remember last Mother's Day when he told me how much he loved me and appreciated having me as his mom. Simple words from a man no longer a boy. Last Mother's Day, I thought about him being a parent someday and how good he would be. Last Mother's Day, I realized the bulk of my work was done. He was a man now and would soon be nurturing a life of his own.

But everything has changed. And I simply don't have the words for how this feels.

I have memories that remind me of the gifts of motherhood. I remember those crumpled handmade cards in his knapsack and his sticky hands hugging around my neck, and I realize that I am blessed to have those moments to reflect on.

Brendan is here with me and loves like no other. Having both my sons here physically on Mother's Day to present me with cards and flowers and such is not really what the day is about at all. The best gift for me each and every Mother's Day is the moment it allows for reflection on the blessings of motherhood.

The true gift on Mother's Day is seeing that your children are the gifts.

This morning, I am thankful for the gifts of my children. Both so very different in many ways and exactly alike in others, they transformed me from a girl to a woman to a mother. They show me each and every day that it is the little things in life that matter. It is the crumbled cards at the bottom of a crumb-filled knapsack. It is the pictures drawn and proudly displayed on the refrigerator. It is the cuddles and the comfort. They've shown me it is worth the effort, every second, every minute, even when loving so hard hurts sometimes . . .. . it is all worth it. They've shown me that it is indeed all about the love, it always has been, and it always will be. They have shown me that the passage between life and death changes none of that. I began my day by having a silent conversation with my children, much like the quote says:

The best conversations with mothers always take place in silence, when only the heart speaks.

~Carrie Latet~

Today, I am thankful for my children.

May 11th: Going with the Flow

Life is a series of natural and spontaneous changes. Don't resist them; that only creates sorrow . . . Let things flow naturally forward in whatever way they like.

~Lao Tzu~

From early on in my grief journey, I described my decision to grieve with gratitude as a decision to not swim against the current of my life. As I looked at my life with an open and broken heart, I realized I could not swim back upstream to change my circumstances, no matter how much I wished I could. So, I did not resist, and I went with the flow of my life and used gratitude to keep me in the present moment.

Today I am thankful for going with the flow. And I'm glad I wore my life vest.

May 12th: Be Like the Little Engine

I think I can, I think I can. . ..

~Watty Piper (from The Little Engine That Could*)~*

May is a freaking long month. I'm not sure I will make it. So, I am just going to fake it till I make it. I am going to keep writing about resilience and courage and all that other crap until I start to believe it again.

I am going to keep telling myself that I am resilient. A resilient life can only be found if you are looking for it. Resilient people are not born that way. They are carved out of sorrow and pain and hurt.

Today I am thankful for *The Little Engine That Could* . . . he made it over the mountain, and so will I . . .

I am also thankful for quotes like this one:

Stars may be seen from the bottom of a deep well, when they cannot be seen from the top of the mountain. So are many things learned in adversity, which the prosperous man dreams not of.

~Anonymous~

May 15th: A Special Commencement Message

You are educated. Your certification is in your degree. You may think of it as the ticket to the good life. Let me ask you to think of an alternative. Think of it as your ticket to change the world.

~Tom Brokaw~

Today is a special day.

Today is graduation day for North Carolina State University. Today, many of Stephen's beautiful friends will be starting a new chapter in their lives and will be celebrating the special milestone of college completion. And if life had not changed, today would have been Stephen's graduation day. Who knows, maybe it still is. There's no reason why you can't have a cap and gown ceremony in heaven, right?
In any case, on this very special day, I've been thinking about what Stephen would say today if he had the opportunity. I suppose in many ways that's what I've been writing about all along.

If Stephen was here today, I believe that he would tell his fellow graduates:

Drink up every moment. Live like there is no tomorrow. Give it everything you have, even if it seems like it may not pay off. Take chances, stop to smell the roses. Really listen to people when they are talking to you, especially the children you will eventually have. Give back and understand that opening your heart to others is the only way to live life to the fullest. Give love freely, and don't hold back because you're afraid to be hurt.

Understand the true meaning of power. You now officially have those letters behind your name, giving you a professional designation. Congratulations. Use those letters to work professionally, but don't let them become who you are. The number of letters you have behind your name does not make you smart. The title on your office door does not make you powerful. Understand that a truly powerful person is someone who knows that you don't need to be better than anyone and who sees the potential in everyone.

Don't grow up. Today is all about growing up, right? The cap, the gown, and transitioning into the adult world of work, of mortgages and responsibility and becoming a contributing member of society? But here's the secret. You will have to become more responsible, but you don't have to grow up. Keep your enthusiasm for life, act silly, look at life with the wonder of a child. Keep seeing the magic because it is all around you. Your ability to see the magic is one of the biggest pieces of living a life of joy.

Don't settle. There will be people and situations in your life that will present you with a choice. The choice will be to believe in the greatness of who you are or the greatness of someone or something else. Believe in yourself. Don't settle. Don't assume that this is all there is. Because the possibilities for you are endless. Don't stop believing that all of your dreams can come true, and you deserve to have them. Because they can come true, and you deserve it all.

Focus on the similarities instead of the differences. This goes for race, religion, politics, friendships, marriages, laundry detergent, ketchup—you name it. Judging people based on how they differ from you closes your mind and heart to the possibilities of this world. Understand that the greatest strength comes from diversity. Embrace that, and you will hold the strongest energy force in your hands.

Don't let anyone else define you. This is a big one, because it is something that can break your spirit. Don't let anyone define who you are—not because of your mistakes or your accomplishments. Don't let yourself be defined by a moment in your life, ever. Understand that your life is based on all of it, and only God sees the whole picture of who you are, inside and out.

Approach your life with an attitude of gratitude and love. This is another biggie. Because sometimes, life is going to deal you a big old crate of lemons. Approach your life with gratitude, and you will see abundance, even when things are not going so great.

Learn how to forgive. This should have been a required course to graduate. Forgiving will be one of your hardest lessons, but you must learn it if you want to have a fulfilled life. It is not easy, especially when the hurt runs deep. But you need to know how to forgive if you want to be happy.

Understand that life is imperfect, and that is okay. Things rarely go as planned. That is part of the journey. Don't look at your life as a mix of problems and solutions. Because some problems have no solutions. They are simply there in your life to teach you. Trying to find a solution for everything will only leave you feeling like a failure. Make peace with the perfection of imperfection.

Look around, into the faces of your fellow graduates, and know this: If you are still on this earth, there is a reason. You have a purpose, and your job is to discover it. Go out into this world and make a difference. Know that you have the power within each of you to do wonderful things. Believe it.

I believe that is what he would tell us today, confident in his words, speaking his truth. My heart is literally breaking today. But I am still thankful. I am grateful that I raised a boy who would have said and believed every word.

Happy Graduation, Stephen.

May 18th: The Dark of Night

It's not an easy journey, to get to a place where you forgive people. But it is such a powerful place, because it frees you.

~Tyler Perry~

Today, I had planned to go to Stephen's Facebook page and spend some time with my boy. I've been to his page a number of times before today but could never stay long. I would visit and then go away, usually to crawl into my bed, curl up in a ball, and have a good cry before continuing with my day.

I promised myself that I would take care of this before his birthday on May 22nd. I would go in and save some of the special posts, quotes, information, and pictures and then disable his account. I could not have his list of friends be reminded to wish him a Happy Birthday. I've been putting this off long enough, hesitating because it is just one more thing that makes this all final. Once I do this, it is one more piece of him that will dissipate into the atmosphere.

But what I knew was going to be a grueling day turned out to be much, much worse. Because when I went to his Facebook page, it had already been archived. Someone had, without even asking me, notified Facebook that he was dead, and they took it all away, leaving the saddest profile picture of the Marquee lights for the Band of Horses concert he attended two weeks before he died.

It was all gone. It was all flipping gone.

Now, I am sure someone who has not lived my life for the last 10 months would not understand. But this has completely derailed me.

I frantically signed out and then signed back in, refreshed the page 100 times, banged the keyboard, and then burst into tears. I paced around the house and then came back to my laptop to do the same ritual at least 10 more times. It was still all gone. I emailed Facebook and explained the situation and received a "too bad, so sad" email in reply. If I wanted the information, I should call a lawyer.

I am his mother! I am his mother!

In the early hours of July 5th, I relinquished control, and my heart broke. But this, it was honestly just as hurtful because someone, without so much as a thought for me, took this away from me. They took it away from me.

And at that moment, I felt like I was slipping off the edge of the earth, falling into the dark depths of hell. I stepped outside in the warm Carolina sunshine and sat back in the lounger.

I did not notice the blue sky or the chirping birds. I did not see the spring blossoms or smell the freshly cut grass. Instead, I gritted my teeth and clenched my fists and felt my entire world get darker by the minute. It was at that moment that I began to pray.

"Please, God, take the bitterness away. Please, God, don't let this stay with me."

Just as I did on the morning of July 5th, all I could manage was a simplistic mantra, begging for some reprieve. Begging for rescue.

And, about two hours later, it started to come. I will carry this hurt with me a long time, but I will forgive whoever decided to once again take away my power to say goodbye to Stephen on my own terms.

One day. But not today.

Today I am thankful for prayers, curse words, and forgiveness.

May 22nd: On Your Birthday . . .

*If tomorrow morning the sky falls . . . have clouds for breakfast. If you have
butterflies in your stomach . . . ask them into your heart. If you're afraid of
the dark . . . remember the night rainbow.*

~Cooper Edens~

May 22nd.

This is the day that my life changed forever 24 short years ago. This
is the day that, as a young girl in a delivery room, I said goodbye to
Stephen's brother Matthew and hello to a tiny little Stephen. This is
the day I began to learn that parenthood is a gift, a privilege that
most of us don't realize is the biggest and most important thing we
will do on this earth.

Each May 22nd every year since, we have celebrated Stephen and his plain old "awesomeness." There was always a lot to celebrate. That has not changed this year, although I must admit, for this occasion girl, the celebration will be through tears. This is a tough one for me, and this entire week has been mixed with moments where I just felt as if I may fall apart.

But it is his birthday, and I want to celebrate him. I wrote this poem in the early days of July 2009, when I felt as if I may split at the seams because of the pain that sat within my broken heart. I think it captures who he was . . .

You just had this way . . .

I remember . . .

I remember you small and frail, lying on my chest, curled up and comfortable, accepting of me as the provider of safety for you and your little heart. You were so, so tiny, with transparent skin, and delicate and breakable fingers and toes. I remember the late-night feedings, with everyone else asleep, and you, the old soul, looking into my eyes, your own eyes as dark as ebony and deep as the ocean. You barely blinked, and just looked at me and we had this wordless conversation. We talked with our eyes about missing your brother, and the future, and what I wanted for you and for myself. We talked about love in the simplest of conversations. The kind that only a mother and her baby can have in the wee hours of the morning, when the night is stepping back, making room for the dawn to step on stage. It was as if you knew, from the beginning, and could see within my soul. You knew me like no other.

I remember thinking that you were special, different from the rest. You had this way.

I remember you, doing a little dance in the doorway when I would arrive home, missing me as much as I missed you. You had this dancing style that oozed unbridled happiness. I remember the cuddles at bedtime, and the story book, Ordinary Amos and the Amazing Fish. You loved that book so much and never tired of hearing about how Amos was caught by the fish instead of the other way around. You always smiled and acted surprised, even though we had read it a thousand times before. I still have that tattered book, and I read it this morning, aloud, and with the same inflection and enthusiasm I used when I would read it to you. I cried.

I remember thinking you were special, somehow different from the rest. You had this way.

I remember the quiet questions you would ask at bedtime, or in the morning when we would talk quietly, still only half awake. They were questions about the earth, and how we treat each other, and why people were mean to each other because they were different. I remember wondering how you were so wise as a child, when your mother had so much to figure out. I remember you, a little older, looking at me with hurt in your eyes, looking into my own hurt eyes, and neither of us knew how to make it better. I remember seeing the tears in your eyes and vowing I would never let you hurt like that again. I remember you bringing in your first girl to meet me. You were nervous and so was she, and you fumbled your words and laughed nervously. You kept looking at her, and batting your eyelashes, and you laughed in a way I had never heard before. Young love laughter, a mix of excitement, and hormones and anxiety.

I remember thinking that you were special, different from the rest. You had this way.

I remember the look on your face as you drove across the bridge, over the Mississippi River. You were growing up; we were on our big adventure. Laughing and singing to the tunes on the radio and ready for a fresh start. We had so much fun together driving across the country. You had this way. I remember the moment you put the car in reverse, to drive off to university. I remember what you were wearing, those sneakers I never liked but you loved. I remember how excited you were, and how you had everything in order and prepared. I remember you looking up, then putting the car in park, and coming back to hug me and tell me you loved me when you saw me crumbling and falling apart when the car started to pull away.

I remember thinking that you were special, different from the rest. You had this way.

I remember when you grew up, the moment where you transformed; you were no longer a boy, but a man, fantastic and caring and loving man, who would make an enormous difference in this world. You were home, and we were having dinner, and having regular conversation. And I looked at you, and realized you were all grown up, and had turned out better than I ever could have hoped for. We had survived the hormone years, and the teenage angst, and the hurts of the past and the roller coaster ride of having a young mom who was learning as she went along, and you turned out just fine. More than fine. I remember looking at you, and realizing that you were quietly confident and happy, and sure of yourself and what you had to offer.

I remember thinking that you were special, different from the rest. You had this way.

I remember the moment I received the call. I remember the kick in the gut pain. I remember the weird calmness as I drove through the night to get to you. It was like you were with me. Yes, you were with me, and that is why I was calm. I remember knowing that everything had changed. I remember negotiating with God, and how surreal it was to know with certainty that I would be glad to die in your place. I remember the mix of hurt, and pain, and anger and disappointment when I knew God could not change this now. I remember talking with Him, and telling Him that you had this way about you, you were different than the rest . . . and pleading with him to change this . . ..

I remember thinking that you were special, different from the rest. You had this way.

I remember you had this way. This way of being a son that I could never take credit for teaching you. You had this way of taking care of people, of loving people, of making others feel good about themselves and life. You had this way, this invincible way. I would watch you and think that nothing could touch you. I would see you and see perfection and feel like I had contributed something good to this world.

I remember that you had this way of living . . . in the moment and to the fullest. It made your untimely death both unbearable and a little easier to bear all at the same time. You used it all up; you did not waste a moment. But I wonder, about what would have been, the moments that could have followed . . ..

You just had this way, and I was so excited to see how your story was going to unfold.

I remember, and I understand now. You had this way, and that made all the difference to your life. You lived a happy and grateful life, no matter what the circumstance.

My son, my teacher . . . . . . you just had this way.

Happy Birthday to Stephen and Matthew.

Today I am thankful that for the first time, two brothers are celebrating their birthday together. I know it will be a special one.

June 18th: It Truly is the Little Things

The most important things in life aren't things.

~Anthony J. D'Angelo~

It's hard to believe, but June is flying by . . .. . and before you know it, it will be July 4th.

One year.

365 days.

It's hard for me to believe, really, that a year has passed already. In some ways, it seems like only days ago that I answered my cell phone to have the sheriff on the other end tell me that my life would never be the same. But in other ways, it seems like the world slowed a little so that I could experience every moment and write about it, even through my tears. Of all the things I have been most grateful for over the past 11 months, I can surely say that my decision to grieve with gratitude would be at the top of the list.

It has helped me find my way through, allowing me to see the goodness that remains around me. That goodness comes in many forms—people, hugs, and cuddles . . . big brown dogs, flowers, butterflies, tears, laughs, pictures, emails, chocolate icing. None of the things that I've been grateful for were elaborate. In fact, very few of them have been material things at all.

That's my lesson for today. Don't complicate things by looking for the earth-shattering changes in my life. Instead, look at the life I have right now, only with grateful eyes.

June 20th: Memories of My Father

My father didn't tell me how to live; he lived, and let me watch him do it.

~Clarence Budington Kelland~

My dad was amazing. I've been thinking about him for days now, reflecting on him and who he was. In fact, I've been reflecting on the combination of my parents and how they deserve the credit for the way I've grieved loss, being the best teachers in my life. My mother was resilient and able to continue on, no matter what storm she faced in life. My dad believed and proved you can do anything you put your mind to . . . Dad showed me that "where there's a will, there's a way."

He had this swagger when he walked. It was a walk with purpose. When I was older, he told me he'd had an accident at work that had crushed one of his legs, and the doctors said he would never walk the same again, with one leg slightly shorter than the other. He told them he would. And he did. It was that moment I realized that the swagger was more important than I had ever understood.

He could whistle like no other. He had this vibrato in his tone, and he could make music with any song. I can still hear him whistling as he worked around our house, sounding like a beautiful bird.

When he was mad, he said very little. That was left to Mom. But if you really crossed the line, he would point his right crooked index finger at you. His eyes would widen, and he would point. And no words were necessary. I would want to ground myself and take away my allowance. I remember him pointing like that when he found me running around the front lawn with his Knights of Columbus 4th Degree regalia on, plumed hat and cape flowing in the wind, swinging his sword for all the neighborhood kids to see.

He loved my mother and was so protective of her and his children. I never understood truly the depth of the love he had for her until the day I walked into their bedroom and saw him singing to Mom as she lay quietly, dying from cancer. "Blue Moon" . . .. He showed me the kind of love that was possible.

He loved, as did my mother, to have the house full, music playing, and guests to entertain. They were both so good at it. He had a flare for the dramatic and would don costumes, have theme parties, and make moments into memories. He especially loved parades and would have all of his grandchildren parade through the house with an instrument to entertain the masses.

At gatherings at our house, when the guitars would break out, he would always play his tin whistle. This would be a fond memory if only he had known how to play it. He didn't. He would play along, and it sounded like a duck with a vocal injury had snuck into the house and was calling for help.

He would not accept that something could not be fixed. And most times, he was right. He would tinker and work on an appliance until it sputtered its last breath. He wouldn't give up easily. One year, my mother, exasperated with the daily fixes of the washing machine, ordered one from the local store, telling the salesperson it must be delivered before dad got home from work. I believe he would still say he could have fixed the old one. He did not see things as broken. He saw them as waiting to be fixed.

He was an artist but never believed it.

He always made me believe that he really did love the jug of Aqua Velva I gave to him each Christmas.

When he found out I was pregnant with Stephen, he came into my room and sat down on my bed and held my hand and told me everything was going to be just fine. We would work everything out. He told me he loved me through tear-filled eyes. There were no dramatics, no yelling—just love.

Every Christmas Eve, we would have our day, shopping together for last-minute things and perhaps to also give my mother time to clue up preparations at home. We would have lunch together at the same restaurant, my dad would order a cheeseburger, fries, and ice cream and tell me this was our little secret, his cheating on his diet. Each December 24th, I long for those shopping trips and cheeseburgers.

He influenced not only me but Stephen. Stephen had many qualities I could not take credit for. Shortly after Stephen died, I found dad's whistle in Stephen's knapsack, and I realized that he carried my dad with him as much as I did.

Today, I am thankful for my father, who taught me that there is nothing that can break me, nothing that I can't fix, and no limits on the amount of love that can exist in your family.

June 23rd: Sour Milk

Dream as if you'll live forever. Live as if you'll die today.

~James Dean~

This morning, my son and I were chatting in the kitchen. I was packing his lunch for hockey camp, and he was pouring himself a glass of milk to wash down his peanut butter toast. We were chatting and laughing, and then I saw him stop in his tracks.

He was looking at the milk and then quietly said,

"The milk . . . . . .It expires on the same day as Stephen died."

His words caught in his throat and made this mother stop in her tracks on a sunny morning. You see, we knew July 4th was coming. We've talked about it as a family and with our grief counselor. We've made a plan, and we know what we will be doing on that day. But there was something about that darn milk announcing it.

Our family is only a jug of milk's lifespan away from being without Stephen for a full year. There is something about that reality that hits us both as we stare at the skim milk in the glass, almost like the white liquid is the sand of time itself.

So, we talk about it, over milk and peanut butter. We both think Stephen would not want us to focus on the day we lost him, but rather look at all the days we had him. We know we will always think about July 4th differently, but we also know that it is our choice whether we make it a hard day or one of celebration.

Later in the day, as we are in the kitchen preparing for dinner, my husband, after hearing something on the news, exclaims he can hardly believe that it has been a year since the loss of Michael Jackson. He asks me, "Can you believe a year has passed already?"

Yes and no. Yes, I can believe it has been a year because I watched the coverage *with* Stephen, and we both talked at length about the lack of dignity that was given to this poor man in his last hours of life.

Nine days later, I was the parent sitting behind the yellow tape, devastated, and broken open by life. And although the coverage of my loss was in no way comparable to the media circus surrounding Michael Jackson, I had my own taste of the disregard shown to the bereaved, having to read things about Stephen and the accident that implied and judged incorrectly.

But no, I could not believe it has been a year, because in many ways, I can't believe that much time has passed already. I can't believe that I am a jug of milk's lifespan away from a full year.

Last year, as I sat and watched "Entertainment Tonight" with Stephen, we talked about this family in Hollywood and the tragedy that they faced. We discussed it as onlookers to their pain, never once contemplating that we could ever experience anything like it.

And now, 11 months later, I'm watching the milk in the fridge as the fat-free liquid counts down the last days of the toughest but most awake year of my life.

We are not as fortunate as the milk. The bottom of my foot does not bear an expiration date.
None of us knows when it will be our time to go. Unlike the milk, the future is not as certain for us. It could come after many years of living, or it could come tomorrow as we mow the lawn.
That is why we must live each moment like it is our last.

Today, I am thankful for sour milk. Making it real for me.

June 27th: You've Got One Week to Fit It All in . . .

I don't want to get to the end of my life and find that I have just lived the length of it. I want to have lived the width of it as well.

~Diane Ackerman~

I am thinking a lot about this time last year. I am starting to lament about the time leading up to July 4th, which will mark a full 365 days that Stephen has been in heaven. It seems a little surreal as I type it. In many ways, the past year has felt like an eternal journey of never-ending hurt. In others, it has been the most awake year of my life and one I am grateful for. My world was forever changed almost a year ago, and it has been a double-edged sword. I miss him: three words that I have quietly uttered repeatedly as I cried over my keyboard, writing away the pain. I gaze up to his picture, his beautiful smile frozen in time and with a guttural sound, I simply say, "I miss you" as I hold my chest.

I find that as I approach the day, I have a range of emotions. It is difficult to describe really, to be a bystander to the passage of time.

I've written hundreds of thousands of words in a year. The words have flowed from me, and I often wonder if it is me writing the words or if I am the virtual assistant to the universe. I'm glad that I decided to grieve this way. I can see it provided me with a thread to hold onto . . . . . when I felt like I may be at the end of my rope without a knot in sight. Many days, many words sparked a reflection in me that saved me from myself, protected me from bitterness, and allowed me to keep living.

With each passing day, I am noticing my focus is shifting. I am beginning to write not so much about death and grief but about life and living. And as I shift, I am finding that one cannot exist without the other, and the relationship between the two is what adds the season, the flavor in our very existence. Because the life I have now is much deeper and richer than it ever has been before. I appreciate my life, my family, and my surroundings more because of the loss in my life. I have perspective.

So, as part of that perspective, I am thinking about this time last year. Stephen had a week to live.

7 days.

Any one of us could be in a position like Stephen was this time last year, beginning the last week of our life on earth. What if the clock was ticking, our number was going to be called, and the time had come? What if this was it? What if God sent a text message and gave a heads up to clue up some things before pickup?

What would you do on your bucket list?

Who would you contact to say, "I love you"?

Who would you call to say, "I'm sorry"?

What foods would you eat?

What books would you read?

How would you change how you parent your children?

Would you make any changes in your relationships? With your partner? Your friends? Your siblings? Yourself?

What fears would you throw out the window?

What adventures would you fit into the seven days?

Would you focus on what you've lost or what you have?

What kind of conversation would you have with God to make sure all your affairs were in order?

I think I've just created the Instruction Manual for my life. And I think I am supposed to live it.

I am surrounded by a million one little things.

July 3rd: If Tomorrow Never Comes . . .

Never bend your head. Always hold it high. Look the world straight in the face.

~Helen Keller~

I don't want tomorrow to come. So, whoever is in charge, stop the earth's rotation. Just give me another few days to get ready for it.

I've been faking all week, smiling through the pain, telling people that Brady, Brendan, and I are going to have a quiet day together. We have been on the road, and if I could be completely honest, I am trying to find the roadmap for the end of the earth so we can drive there. I want to get away, as far away from the Fourth of July as I possibly can. No fireworks, no hot dogs, no American flags, or musical interludes of "God Bless America."

I am trying to keep this in perspective. I am trying to refocus on gratitude. But boy, this is tough. So, what am I thankful for on this 364th day?

I have continued to breathe, even when that breath has caught in my tightened throat, constricted with the sudden flashes of reality: he is gone. I have continued to inhale, even when I just thought it would be easier and less painful if I did not. I've continued to suck in air, even when I begged God to take my breath away and give it to Stephen.

My heart has continued to beat, even though it is broken open and in a million pieces. And more than just beat, it has continued to fill with love each day. And in the wreckage, there is a special room where Stephen sits with me, each day, urging me on to live and to be happy.

I am thankful for the memories that have surfaced because of this terrible event. I have visited places in my past I had long forgotten, and it has been a wonderful trip. This journey has been so much more than grieving for Stephen. It has been a reflection on my lifetime since that glorious and imperfect night in 1986.

I am thankful for the glimpses of happiness: the cuddles with Brendan, the swims, the beach, the friends, the family. In the first moments, I thought my life was destined for perpetual darkness. I now know that is not true. The glimpses have given me hope, much like someone worn out from a weeklong weather system of rain and cloud, only to be treated with 20 minutes of bright and beautiful sunshine. The warmth and light radiate over your face, and you remember the glory of the blue sky. And at minute 21, the clouds reform and the warmth will dissipate, but you know the sunshine is still there behind a cloud. It will come back. So, thank you for the glimpses of my life of sunshine. I have hope, and I know the skies will be blue again.

I am thankful for the love that resides in my heart and in my house. I am at peace knowing that Stephen's last days were filled with love—that deep and unconditional love that never judges, never expects anything in return but simply endures. I am thankful for that, and I intend to pay that love forward. I feel I have a big portion here in my heart, his share, if you will. I am excited for what I am about to embark on, sharing that love with those who need it.

I am thankful for Stephen—an unconventional start, middle, and ending but a wonderful life just the same. I am so, so grateful for him, and for the 23 years I did have with him. I cannot imagine where I would be in life without his influence. He changed me, from the moment I looked into those eyes of his, those old and knowing eyes. He changed me with his life and with his death. I am thankful for him and for all that he gave me and continues to give me through my reflection. I am thankful that so many others were touched by his life as well. I am humbled, silenced, and speechless by the people who have and continue to reach out simply to say he changed them, he affected them, and he loved them and took care of them just how they needed. Every mother should be so lucky to hear the words I have about their child.

Thank you for bringing me to my knees. I am not thankful I lost my son. Of course not. I continue to wish and pray every night that perhaps I could wake up, and this would be a nightmare of epic proportion, and life would be back to normal. I also wish that if that is not possible, then at least let me see him in my dreams. Let me see him smile, hear his laugh, see him run and play.

But as I know that is not possible, I say thank you for bringing me to my knees. It has allowed me to find myself, whom I was beneath the day-to-day stresses, the bills, the material stuff, and the responsibilities, the opinions of others, the gossip, and the baggage. This has stripped my life bare, and I am now rebuilding it according to my terms, knowing what is truly important this time around. I have a renewed sense of wonder at the magic of the world and now have the strength to live a life of purpose. A life that honors who Stephen was and who I finally know I am.

Brought to my knees, I never thought I would stand again. I never thought it would be possible. Some days, I still have fleeting moments of that same feeling. Right now, I only stand part of the time. But the clarity is there. I can appreciate the view when I stand much more, having spent this time on the ground.

July 4th: Parades, Hope in My Pocket, and Remembering Stephen One Year Later

Memory is a way of holding onto the things you love, the things you are, the things you never want to lose.

~From the television show "The Wonder Years"~

I thought I knew exactly what I would write about today. I have, of course, had this day on my mind, wondering how it would play out and whether or not I would fall apart all over again. In some ways, it hardly seems like a day has passed, let alone an entire 365 of them—a full year since that phone call, telling me that life was forever changed. I can hardly believe it in some ways, and in others, I feel as if I have been wandering the earth for years with this heavy wagon pulling behind me, the wagon of grief, filled with rocks—rocks of anguish, ache, pain, loss, sadness, and confusion.

So, in anticipation, I planned where I would be and who would be with me; I thought about what I would write in remembrance of a beautiful life taken too soon. And I planned to be as far removed from the 4th of July celebrations as I possibly could. I did not want anything to do with a hot dog, a flag, a parade, or a fireworks display. It just did not seem to fit with the emotions that are attached to this day for me . . .. the day the world changed.

But, as it's been with most of my grieving, the day is not what I expected. I often think that Stephen has brought me lessons over the last 12 months to both teach me and guide me through the darkest days and reaffirm what is profoundly important. He was always so much smarter than me.

So, the well-prepared, well-thought-out journal entry does not fit anymore.

Because, as I was driving with my husband and son on Maine's Route One, thinking I had successfully outrun the 4th of July, I came upon a roadblock. A police car with flashing lights sat in the middle of the tiny two-lane road, waving us down and instructing us to stop. My immediate reaction was that it was something bad, an accident. It was not — far from it, actually.

It was a parade.

And, at the head of the line of stopped traffic, we had front row seats. For the next hour, we watched fire trucks and ponies, politicians, and local personalities. I watched small children chase after candy as it was thrown from a truck, their parents running behind them to ensure they did not wander too close to the road. I watched families smiling and chatting with one another, taking the time on this sunny day to do what we should all do more of every day: just love each other. It was young faces and old, waving flags and wearing funny hats, just smiling and living life as it should be. And I realized something.

That is as it should be.

I have a theory. I believe Stephen decided we needed to be at the front of the line to watch that parade. I believe he brought us to that remote road on Maine's coastline at that very moment to show us that it is still okay to smile and celebrate the 4th of July. I believe he wanted us to know that we can't outrun the day, nor should we try.

As the parade ended, the police car escorted us through the main street of the town, and we waved to the crowds as if we were the most magnificent part of the parade. Spectators laughed and took our picture and thanked us for coming.

I tried to outrun the 4th, but it found me . . .. and it turns out, that was a good thing.

It seems strange to think that he has been gone for a full year. Because honestly, he has been nestled in my heart this whole time. I feel him with me daily, guiding me, leading me towards a life full of living. I've had hundreds of deep conversations with him, reflecting on life and death. I feel him when I am parked behind a police car watching a parade or when I am driving down a lonely road singing songs from Queen's "Greatest Hits." I feel him when I stop and smell the roses or do something that is not at all grown up or laugh until I snort.

I feel him when I am living.

I spent the last 365 days looking for the good in the worst of situations. There were many days I could have found plenty of excuses to give up, to shut the curtains and wait to die. And some days, that seemed like a better option than to face the unbelievable pain that comes with losing a child, especially one as magnificent as Stephen.

But I didn't. I made a choice to look for the good in life and to choose happiness. It has been the hardest thing I've ever done in my life.

And although it has not always been easy, the decision to approach my life with gratitude has been the greatest gift. Because with a grateful heart, I can feel my beautiful boy all around me every single day.

There has not been a day in the past year that he has not been a constant on my mind. With every decision, every move, every day, I think of him. I believe I will think of him like that until I die.

But until I die, I will live. And that is what this year has taught me. I can both hurt and live at the same time. In fact, I think that is truly what life is supposed to be. It is a mixture of both, a delicate recipe of two ingredients that balance each other, the good and the bad. You can't really truly appreciate the delicate flavor of the goodness in your life until the bitter taste of life's troubles has touched your tongue, reminding you of just how good your life really is.

I thought I would be writing this profound summation of events for this most sacred of days. It turns out the real lesson came in a parade.

Life can still be wonderful, even when it hurts. And that is one little thing.

Happy 4th of July, Stephen . . ..

"Come to the edge," he said. They said, "We are afraid." "Come to the edge," he said. They came. He pushed them. And they flew.

~Guillaume Apollinaire~

Acknowledgments

Without the love and support of many, I would not have been able to put one word to paper. I send special love and gratitude to:

Brady and Brendan. Without you, this journey would not have happened. I was not strong enough to do this alone.

My family and friends, who have loved me through each page.

My best friend, Tracey. We have a rare and beautiful friendship, and I give thanks each morning that you are by my side.

And finally, thanks to the thousands of people who wrote to me after reading *Gratitude in Grief* or my blog. I am honored to have your support and encouragement and feel so incredibly blessed that you trust me with your own stories of gratitude and resilience.

Printed in Great Britain
by Amazon

45017216R00175